RAISING RIGHTEOUS CHILDREN

RAISING RIGHTEOUS CHILDREN

A THIRTY-DAY JOURNEY TO PARENTING WITH
GODLY WISDOM

REV. DR. TERESA ALLISSA CITRO

Book and cover design by eBook Prep: www.ebookprep.com

April, 2021, ISBN: 978-1-64457-233-7

Rise UP Publications
644 Shrewsbury Commons Ave
Ste 249
Shrewsbury PA 17361
United States of America

www.riseUPpublications.com
Phone: 866-846-5123

CONTENTS

With love, I dedicate this book to my amazing, awesome, and most importantly my godly parents, Antonio and Teresa Arcuri, and to my children, Justin Noah and Ellianna Destinee, for being my precious jewels I wear proudly on my crown. You have enriched my life and taught me more by your godly lives.

INTRODUCTION

This book contains godly advice, experience, and skills in parenting, which you should apply to yourself when it is necessary. The Bible says, in Proverbs 22:6, *"Train a child in the way he should go, and even when he is old he will not turn away from it."* This book explains how to raise children in the ways of the Lord.

Amongst the many things we learned about God, discipline was the most important of all lessons. Discipline is a requirement for a child to learn what is right and what is wrong. Growing up, we both learned really quickly what happens when we do wrong. Our mom's advice through Bible teachings taught us what was acceptable and what was not.

In Ephesians 6:1-4, it states, *"Children, obey your parents because you are Christians. This is the right thing to do. Honor your father and mother that everything may go well for you, and you may have a long life on earth."* This is an important commandment with a promise. *"Fathers, don't make your children bitter about life. Instead, bring them up in Christian discipline and instruction."*

Our mother was and is an honorable and respectable role model of a parent, who honors, fears, and serves God. Honor is lacking in the modern household. Children are brought up to dishonor and disobey their parents and teachers. They don't even think about honoring God whatsoever. Our mom provides an excellent example for parents on how to teach their children these key values. God requires us to honor our parents in our day to day actions, and we are and still are being brought up to do so. In Deuteronomy 5:6, it states, *"Honor your father and your mother as the Lord your God has commanded you. Then you will live for a long time, and things will go well for you in the land the Lord your God is giving you."*

Our mom taught us not to be selfish, but to be selfless, and she also taught us to give generously. In her teachings of unselfishness, she taught us to offer our bodies as a living sacrifice to God. Her teachings provided inspiration for us to give generously to others and to God through her own selfless example, according to Philippians 2:4, which states, *"Don't be concerned only about your own interests, but also be concerned about the interests of others."*

Our mother continues to be a shining light and an inspiration to others. She had the boldness and faith to go through trials and tribulations, not only in her children's lives, but also her own. She cared so much about the approval of God that she didn't care what people thought of her. She did not care about what people said. She only cared about what God had to say. She brought up her children to be an image of herself. Our mom is the epitome of a godly parent and what all parents should strive to be like.

If you want to be a successful role model in your children's lives, you should apply all the many teachings in this book to your life and your parenting skills.

We love you Mom, and we're proud of you for your stand for God and for being a godly influence in our lives and in the lives of others.

Justin Noah Citro

Ellianna Destinee Citro

A MOTHER'S PRAYER

As women, the most important job we have is to be a mother and being a mother is an honor given to us by God, who has entrusted us with the most precious gift, our children.

In Psalm 127:13, the Word of God says, *"Children are an inheritance from the LORD. They are a reward from him."* Our children are truly an inheritance and a blessing given to us from the hands of God. Because I genuinely believe this, when my publisher asked me to write a book on prayer, encouragement, and promises to be prayed and spoken over our children, I was excited. I believe strongly in the power of prayer and its effects.

My children, Justin and Ellianna, are miracle babies. I was praying for my children long before they made their entrance into this world. God heard my prayers and brought me two outstanding children. They go far beyond my expectations, and are more awesome than I could ever have imagined. I'm most grateful for the love and reverence they have for God and for me, their mother.

As mothers, we must pray and speak the Word of the living God over the lives of our children, and we must take it very seriously. From the moment my children, Justin and Ellianna, arrived home from the hospital, prayer was a part of our daily lives. There are countless times I have told Justin and Ellianna, "I only speak God's Word!" I still say those words to them.

I am giving thanks to God for the work He is doing in the lives of my children. My son, Justin, began Bible college and seminary this year and is majoring in theology and counseling. His desire is to preach the Word of God and counsel people in the ways of the Lord. My daughter, Ellianna, just turned 13, and she has been writing since she was seven years old. She has been encouraging children to follow God. God has blessed me by allowing me to see them live their lives out loud and unashamed to stand up for Christ and to proclaim His Gospel. They are testimonies of the greatness of our God, bringing honor to Him and me, and they will be passing the Gospel of Jesus Christ to their children, and then to the generations to come. A life fully lived out for Christ is something that we, as parents, should aspire to pass on to our children above all else.

God clearly states, *"Children are an inheritance!"* This Bible verse is very significant, and it is such a powerful statement. Our children represent us. I always say to my children when we go places, or when they leave my presence, "Remember who you are. You are representing my name, and my name is precious and honored. Keep it that way!"

They know I mean business. You see, we are leaving a legacy for them to follow. They are inheriting who we are and what we stand for. They inherit what we have taught them. They have a birthright, and we have to be sure we are showing them how important and powerful their birthright truly is. There is a heritage they will bring forth. That heritage must not be spoiled. We are passing down an important heritage of blessings that they will pass down to their children and future generations.

There is a precious richness in honoring the Word of God and seriously taking His inheritance to our children. We must be careful that cultural traditions never overtake God's Word. We must guide with wisdom, love, patience, endurance, encouragement, and with an attitude of never giving up no matter what they do. We have been given the power to govern well and protect our children against all harm.

"They are a reward from him." God rewards those who look for Him. He makes His perfect will come to pass in their lives. God wants us to raise families that bring honor and glory to Him. He wants the world to see that His people are blessed. He says, *"Children are a reward,"* and we must treasure these precious lives He has bestowed upon us to raise with love and understanding, not with an iron rod of rules and regulations without explanations. We are to guide our children well, and we must guide with love. We must constantly explain what is right and wrong, and we must share with them the blessings they will receive for obeying God with their whole heart. God said, *"They are a reward."* This means He has honored us with our beautiful children. When we are honored with a precious gift, we maintain it close to our heart, and we protect it. How

much more should we honor the beautiful lives of our children?

Our children are the greatest presents God could bestow upon our lives. They are precious in His sight, and they are to be held very tightly by us, not to control but to protect. As parents, we are to light their way by the lives we live for Christ. When God says 'reward,' it means more than just giving us a gift. This reward means a payment of their lives, and they will pay us back by how they live their lives. Therefore this will affect their lives and the perfect and good plans God has prepared for them in advance, we need to do our utmost to help shape and form them to bring forth those gifts God has given them.

These short prayers, encouragement, and promises to be prayed over your children will bring you, as a mother, before the throne room of God, the God who has entrusted you to bring up your children in His Word and for His glory. God is going to listen to the prayers of a righteous person, and God is going to hear your prayer for your children. Your children will be blessed, and you shall be called blessed. As the Word of God says,

"Her children rise up and call her blessed!"

— PROVERBS 31:28 ESV

DAY 1: DISCIPLINE IS IMPORTANT

"God corrects you as a father corrects his children.
All children are disciplined by their fathers."

— HEBREWS 12:7

God identifies Himself as a father towards us, and He expects us to correct and discipline our children. He goes on to say, *"All children are disciplined by their fathers."* In other words, a good father will discipline (teach) his children in the right way to go. Notice how He is saying, "All?" You see, all children are learning either godly behavior and attitudes or ungodly behaviors and attitudes.

We cannot afford to not allow ourselves to discipline. Parenting children is not an easy job. We have challenging days, and sometimes, children will do what they want to do. Our job is always to discipline lovingly. We are to tell our children that we love and believe in them. They already have it in them to do what is right because God has given us all a moral compass; however, we need to learn how to use it.

The moral compass is our conscience. If we don't teach this to our children, then we will have failed. We need to explain that when we disobey, we are setting ourselves up for colossal failure. If we don't teach this to our children, then we have failed.

APPLICATION:

Both of my children, after punishing them, will come to me days later and tell me, "Mom, I am sorry. I deserved punishment." My children are genuinely sad when they fail me. I cannot tell you how many times, after their punishments, my children want me to hug and kiss them, and as I'm hugging them, they break out into tears.

Ellianna once said, "Mommy, I am crying because I feel bad that I disappointed you. I do not want my technology back. I feel so bad and ashamed." I was quick to hug her back, hold her, wipe her tears away, and tell her, "Ellianna, I love you and your brother way too much to see you destroyed by poor choices that you two make. I am your mother, and no one will ever love you more except for God. It is my job to discipline you and your brother. I take this job very seriously. I am not your killjoy. I am a mother who loves you deeply. I know what is in you, and I will not allow Satan to steal it from you. You guys have a mother who will do anything to help you, and I am like a lioness watching over you. Let me do my job and do it well before our God."

Honesty is a good thing to practice with your children. I find that explaining to them why I discipline while I am punishing them is a good thing. No child takes punishment with joy and delight. Just be prepared for the outbursts and the ignoring they will do after the punishment. It's okay. They are children, and they act that way because they are children. You just do your job and do it well.

PRAYER:

Heavenly Father, You are the greatest parent there is, and I am coming to You in need of the wisdom and understanding that comes from You, to know how to guide and discipline my children correctly.

My desire is to be the mother You want me to be so I may bring honor to You in how I discipline the children You have blessed me with and entrusted into my care.

Help me show them that You, O God, are a loving Father who corrects us with love.

Let me always point my children to You in how I correct them so that they may see You as their Father in Heaven, even after I am gone.

In Jesus' name, Amen.

THINK ABOUT IT:

What practical ways can you implement discipline for your children in this area?

Write out a prayer, specifically for your children, about this area of discipline.

DAY 2: DISCIPLINE MATTERS TO GOD

> *"If you are not disciplined—and everyone undergoes discipline—then you are not legitimate, not true sons and daughters at all."*

— HEBREWS 12:8

I broke down this passage in Hebrews 12 because it is so vital to discipline. Discipline is at the core of God's heart, and as we learned in the previous verse, He is saying that all fathers discipline. He never said, "A good or bad father." He said, *"All children are disciplined by their fathers."* He is expecting us to discipline. Here, God is getting down to the core of it. I always felt horrible knowing that they didn't have parents who disciplined them,

I have been a youth leader in three churches. I have seen it all. I knew right away which kids would make it and those that wouldn't. I saw more children destroyed by the lack of discipline, and I can't tell you how many students told me they wished I was their mother. This was never a compliment to me. I always felt horrible knowing they didn't have parents who disciplined them, keeping them from making huge mistakes.

Sometimes, parents want to be their children's friends. Please, parents, you were not called to be your children's friends. You were called to be their parents. Parents have responsibilities towards their children. They cannot see you as a friend. A friend is on your children's levels, this is why you can't be friends.

You have to have the authority given to you by God Himself to govern your home well. Children want these guidelines in place. They thrive on it. It keeps their boundaries and barriers in check. They know Mom and Dad will not be happy if they do something to upset them. It gives them the push they need to behave and not have to pay the consequences. Children will push you to the limit, and you must rise to the occasion to make godly decisions on the spot.

APPLICATION:

My children push me, too. I have this saying when they push me: "You are pushing me to the limit, and I am there. I suggest you stop. Halt right where you are. If you continue to push me, I will rise to the occasion, and you will not like it." I even hold up my hand before them. They know to not go beyond that.

My daughter loves animals, and since we were on vacation in Florida, I had purchased tickets to SeaWorld, her favorite place to go, two days before we were going to leave.

She was talking back to me, and I had given her plenty of warnings to stop. I warned several more times, and then I disciplined her. Even with the tickets in hand, I told her, "No, your punishment will be not going to SeaWorld."

Oh, the crying that took place! However, I had to discipline. It cost me money, and the tickets were not returnable. We stayed at the hotel and didn't go to SeaWorld. My daughter was so upset, but she never did it again. Kids learn, and sometimes, it costs us something. It cost the SeaWorld tickets for my daughter. Money is nothing if you lose your children.

PRAYER:

Heavenly Father, Your love is what I want to model for my children. I refuse to be a parent who does not correct their children. Because I love my children, I will do whatever it takes to discipline them.

Lord, help me to discipline them the correct way, and let me punish in a way that makes them stop and think about the consequences of their actions and choices.

Father, I am not punishing just to punish them, instead I am punishing with intent to help my children grow in the area of their weakness, bringing them to the place of blessings.

Father, let my children learn from their mistakes and let them make wise decisions next time. Lord, I ask that You let my children grow in wisdom so that they will not make terrible mistakes which will cost them their future, and Father, give me the grace I need to discipline and parent with bold determination. In Jesus' name, Amen.

THINK ABOUT IT:

What practical ways can you implement discipline for your children in this area?

Write out a prayer, specifically for your children, about this area of discipline.

DAY 3: PARENTS MUST LEARN TO DISCIPLINE

*"Correct your son, and he will give you peace of
  mind. He
will bring delight to your soul."*

— PROVERBS 29:17

W e must learn to discipline our children according to the Word of God and to the law of the land. I have disciplined my children by taking away technology. In addition, they had to search God's Word to find out about what God has to say about the wrong they committed.

For example, if they disobeyed, I asked them to look in Scripture for verses on disobedience, and they had to give me a report on why it was wrong and what they learned. If they knew what the Word of God had to say, then I asked them, "What do you think the punishment needs to be for what you did? What would you do if you were the parent?"

I saw their little faces of regret, horror with tears coming down their faces. It was wonderful for me because I knew God was speaking to my children, and I knew my children were listening.

Parents, we must parent properly. A lack of proper discipline will set up children for great failure. We are not just teaching discipline in that moment for what they did to us, but we are teaching discipline for a lifetime. They need to learn how to discipline themselves to keep themselves from doing what is wrong. It is something that doesn't end as a child.

APPLICATION:

When my son was 10 years old, he refused to do his math. I was getting angrier by the moment. Finally, I prayed to God quietly. I will never forget this moment and neither will my son.

God spoke to me in an instant. "Take his brand-new birthday bike away, take it to the Salvation Army, and give it away. Make him put it in the car, and make him take it out of the car and hand it to the Salvation Army himself." I was shocked. Even I was asking God, "It's a brand-new bike, and it cost me $350 dollars. It was specifically customized for Justin. I can't buy another one." God said, "Take it now!"

I obeyed. I can't even tell you what it was like in the car. Justin cried the whole way, begging me to change my mind. God had given me an order, and I couldn't back down.

This bike had a license plate with his name on it. The man at the Salvation Army asked him if he wanted his name tag. Justin took his name tag and hugged it all the way home, crying hysterically.

I kept telling him, "Justin, I love you with all my heart. I am sorry you are hurting, but you rudely refused to do your math. I have warned you repeatedly for months now. You chose to disobey, and you gave me no choice. God got involved. I can't do anything against what God says."

You see, I was modeling obedience to God for Justin, even if I didn't have the money to get him another bike. To this day, Justin still can't find a bike to replace that one! The lesson he learned that day was a big one. He never disobeyed me again when doing his schoolwork.

Today, he is in Bible college and seminary, studying to become a minister of God's Word, majoring in theology and counseling. Go, God!

Never be afraid to discipline. You are teaching, instructing, and directing when you discipline. That is what it means. In addition, you are showing a good code of behavior by using the correct punishments for disobedience.

You must rule in a godly manner with a firm hand, establishing the important code of rules. Showing authority is important, and order is a must.

PRAYER:

Heavenly Father, because You are my Instructor, I ask You to teach me according to Your Word.

I ask for the Holy Spirit to guide me in Your truth as I train my children to know what is right and what is wrong.

Help me to teach them how to change ungodly mindsets in their lives.

Set them apart for Your service, filling them to overflow with Your Holy Spirit.

I pray my children will give me peace of mind and that they will grow in wisdom and delight in Your ways.

In Jesus' name, Amen.

THINK ABOUT IT:

What practical ways can you implement discipline for your children in this area?

Write out a prayer, specifically for your children, about this area of discipline.

DAY 4: WHY WE DISCIPLINE CHILDREN

"Moreover, we have all had human fathers who disciplined us and we respected them for it. How much more should we submit to the Father of spirits and live!"

— HEBREWS 12:9

We discipline because of this Bible verse, *"Moreover, we have all had human fathers who disciplined us..."*

We discipline so that our children understand that they must submit to God Himself. When we are teaching them to submit to God Himself, that is a very important lesson, and also the most difficult to teach because you are going against the sinful nature.

Sinful nature is selfish and self-gratifying. It goes against all of God's holiness. However, disciplining our children is teaching them to submit to God.

God does not play games with us. He loves us too much. We are humans, and we want to make our children happy. However, God is interested in building character, integrity, honor, and holiness in us. He knows that we cannot afford to be undisciplined and be illegitimate as if we are not real children of the people we call Dad and Mom.

When we discipline well, we are respected by our children. God is saying, "You had human parents who disciplined you for your own good." You understand that a good parent disciplines, not out of pleasure, but out of necessity to raise good children who will live good lives and not lives of regret.

I want to be sure that my children will not do anything that will bring them dishonor, disgrace, and lives of misery.

APPLICATION:

After the punishment of not taking my daughter to SeaWorld, I asked her, "What have you learned?" She was 11 years old at the time.

She said, "Mom, I learned that the penalty for my actions is too much, and I learned I have a problem with my mouth. It's like it talks back when I don't want to talk back. You understand, Mom? I didn't mean to be rude or disobedient to you. It was because I didn't know how to shut up."

I couldn't help myself. I broke out laughing hysterically, and I explained to my daughter that I wasn't laughing at her, but rather, I was laughing at our humanity.

I explained that, at her young age, she was wrapping up sin in one simple statement. I then explained how we need to bring into discipline everything that causes us trouble and pain. She lost out on a trip to SeaWorld because of her smart mouth. However, the lesson learned was enormous.

You see, the last part of this verse clearly states, *"We submit to the Father of spirits and live."* Catch this truth, please: to live, we submit to God. Our children need to understand and catch this truth, too. You and I are the ones to teach it.

PRAYER:

Heavenly Father, my desire is for my children to live in perfect harmony with You, the great I Am.

I pray they learn what submission is and how to submit themselves before You. I long for my children to know the power of Your name, and I want them to know that obedience is better than sacrifice. You don't look at the outer appearance; You look at the heart. You don't care about sacrifices, but You do care about obedience and walking humbly before You.

Today, I ask for Your help as I teach my children to be disciplined in their thoughts and actions.

Father, before my children's eyes as they watch me, let me be a living demonstration of how to submit to You and receive life abundantly. As I demonstrate for them what submission is and how to submit, let it sink deep into their hearts so that they may teach it to their generation, their children, and all those who follow after them.

In Jesus' name, Amen.

THINK ABOUT IT:

What practical ways can you implement discipline for your children in this area?

Write out a prayer, specifically for your children, about this area of discipline.

DAY 5: DISCIPLINE IS NOT FUN

"No discipline seems pleasant at the time, but painful. Later on, however, it produces a harvest of righteousness and peace for those who have been trained by it."

— HEBREWS 12:11

W e have spent a lot of time on this topic because it is important to establish discipline and to look closely at the Bible verses on it. I couldn't ignore the importance of each verse from Hebrews 12.

It is very meaningful because it follows Hebrews 11, the great chapter on faith, which speaks of those who God said had great faith. Those people were disciplined, and the time came when they learned to submit to the discipline of God in their lives.

It is clear that no one likes discipline. It is painful. It was made to hurt. It wasn't made to make us happy. It is a time to reflect on what we have done. Later, when we have disciplined our children, they will be grateful for all the lessons we have taught them.

It is from a heart of love that we discipline. I cry when I discipline my children. I know in my heart and mind what I was about to give them, but they disobeyed. I had to decide to take away what they had or were about to receive.

May I pause here for one second to reflect on something very important that the Holy Spirit just whispered into my heart? "It is the same for you."

We do not know what God has for us or our children, and because we excuse, condone, or hide the sins our children commit, we lose the blessings. God says, "No, you are not ready for what I am about to give you. I have to take it away for now."

I wonder what our attitudes would be if we knew what we were about to lose or have taken away. Teaching this to our children is so important. They miss out on the best of the very best, the cream of the crop, when we don't discipline them and when we look the other way.

When we discipline properly, it produces a great harvest in the lives of our children. It produces righteousness and peace in those who have been trained by discipline. Are we training this in our children's lives?

APPLICATION:

I know people who have trained their children well, and now those children are adults and have children of their own.

I'm thinking of one pastor I had. They spent a lot of time with their children. Their children are adults, and one daughter has children of her own. I am friends with all of them. Their daughter and I spent this past summer talking about parenting.

She recalled how her parents disciplined her and how she is so grateful for their godly parenting skills, never allowing her or her siblings to get away with anything. She said, "Teresa, I want to be just like my parents in raising my children."

She's right on! Her parents spent hours on end with them. Monday was their time as a family, even though her father was the lead pastor at a church of 500 people. Monday was dedicated to family, and they did things together as a family, and that has never changed.

Today, they reap the harvest of righteous children who have peace of mind in their own life circumstances. The Crosby kids were trained well. Honor and blessings follow them, and they are a crown on their parents' heads.

PRAYER:

Heavenly Father, You are the God of order.

Help me to always put You first, my spouse second, and my children third.

Let everything I do be done properly and in order.

Father, I choose to be disciplined by You so that I can learn from You how to be the parent You desire me to be. When I have my priorities correct, I know You will bless me.

Help me to do what is right in Your eyes and to seek Your approval. Teach me and show me how to prioritize so I can demonstrate to my children the great love I have for them.

In Jesus' name, Amen.

THINK ABOUT IT:

What practical ways can you implement discipline for your children in this area?

Write out a prayer, specifically for your children, about this area of discipline.

DAY 6: A SMALL WINDOW OF OPPORTUNITY

"They disciplined us for a little while as they thought best; but God disciplines us for our good, in order that we may share in his holiness."

— HEBREWS 12:10

As parents, we have just a small window of opportunity to discipline our children. I'm Italian born and raised. My parents still tell me what to do, and so many times I still obey even if I don't like what they are saying.

My Mom will say, "I am saying this for your own good. Please listen. I still pray and ask God to open your mind to see truth." I thank God for my godly parents.

They were very strict in raising my brothers and me, especially with me being the only daughter. Then, she says, "Your father and I gave every moment, every breath to make sure you and your brothers live a life worthy of the blessings of God." Again, she is right. Her final statement is, "You are an adult now. I can't punish you anymore, but I will surely tell you how wrong you are in this decision. I suggest you listen and change your mind."

Her "little while" went away, and she knows it. We have only a little while as shown to us in this passage, *"They discipline us for a little while as they thought best."*

My parents went beyond their best to discipline us. They were excellent role models of how to be as a father and mother, and I am the recipient of their parenting skills. Thank You, God.

We, as parents, face the same thing. We try to do our best to discipline our children for their own good. Please note the use of "but" in the verse after the mention of our parents disciplining us: *"But, God disciplines us for our good, in order that we may share in his holiness."* Here is the whole purpose—to share in His holiness. Parents, please hear me; it is all about holiness. Holiness is everything, and we must teach it to our children through discipline.

APPLICATION:

I believe in explaining things to our children. I told my children, "Listen, everything you do will either bring God glory or disgrace. If you bring God glory, there are many blessings, and you won't even be able to count them. If you bring disgrace, you have nothing but regrets, shame, and humiliation. What do you want?"

After my daughter, Ellianna, learned her lesson and missed out on the SeaWorld trip, it wasn't until the following year that I took her back to SeaWorld for three months instead of just two days. We took all of the possible behind-the-scenes lessons to learn about the animals. Ellianna got blessed because I saw that she had a change of heart and was saying things like, "Mommy, I wanted to say this, but I kept quiet and thought it to myself because I knew it was wrong, and I asked God to forgive me." Yes!!!

My 11-year-old understood how to discipline herself. She got it. And this, parents, is what we must do; we must discipline, and do it well.

PRAYER:

Heavenly Father, empower me with Your Holy Spirit, and fill me to be overflowing so that I may be productive in the fruit of self-discipline and self-control in all I do and say so that I might effectively instruct and discipline my children in those areas.

Help me to teach these very important lessons to them because I know this will not be easy, but I know that I can do anything through Christ who strengthens me. I ask not only for You to give me the mind of Christ, but I ask that You work in me the attitude of Christ.

Lord, as I raise my children in the fear and knowledge of God, I ask You to help my children to hear Your voice deep inside of them, and I ask for You to show them the Way, the Truth, and the Life.

In Jesus' name, Amen

THINK ABOUT IT:

What practical ways can you implement discipline for your children in this area?

Write out a prayer, specifically for your children, about this area of discipline.

DAY 7: WE ARE OUR CHILDREN'S TEACHERS

"He established written instructions for Jacob's people. He gave his teachings to Israel. He commanded our ancestors to make them known to their children."

— PSALM 78:5

As this passage of Scripture clearly shows us, we are our children's teachers.

God established written instructions for Jacob's people. It is God who gave us instructions to follow, which were established by Him for us.

If we don't teach our children to obey, we are the ones who are out of order, and we cause our children to sin. The Word of God tells us, "Obedience is better than sacrifice." Through His written Word, God established all that was necessary for us to follow. He gave it to all of Israel to follow. He commanded our ancestors to make them known to their children. Therefore, we have no excuse.

If our children do not obey, we have lost them. As parents, we need to teach them to obey. We are charged by God to raise up holy children. This is hard work for sure, but with God's help and His written instructions, we must to do this with the guidance of the Holy Spirit.

Our children must obey God's laws, followed by our own, and the laws of the land. Unruly children are a disgrace. It is not the child's fault; it is the parent's fault.

We can be amazing and great parents, or we can bring up children who will defy God and us. God will honor our labor of love when we parent according to the Word of God; however, if kids see chaos, instability, and compromising, they will not take us seriously.

I don't like manmade rules because they always backfire. Obviously, there are laws and rules of the land, and those we can understand. However, I'm talking about rules that some parents make based on their own ideas and thoughts, and they're not backed up by Scripture. Let me tell you, I have seen plenty of those types of parents. It's sad to say their children are not following God and have made a mess of their lives.

Parents need to be courageous and must stand on the conviction of the Word of God. We do our part, and we leave the rest for God. God honors His people.

APPLICATION:

From day one, my children and I wrote out the rules for obedience. I allowed them to participate in writing the rules according to the Word of God, such as no lying, no stealing, no talking back, listening to what I had to say, and doing what I told them, just to name a few. I explained what is acceptable and not acceptable to me, according to the Bible.

My kids know what they need to do. If they disobey, there are consequences. That means they get their stuff taken away.

When they were little, they took out their little lists, and I asked them, "Ok, what do we do now?" They knew the punishment was coming, and they unhappily handed me their toys or their electronic devices, but with regret on their faces. Let me tell you, this is exactly what we need to teach. You see, when you have them write it down with your help, they know what to do.

Kids are a lot smarter and more manipulative than we give them credit for. We need to help them channel their brilliance and use their influence to do greater things. We must help them take the negatives and turn them into positives. We can do this. It must be done with our knees on the ground, praying, asking God to give us wisdom.

My children always gave me lots of material to work with, but I always saw what God was doing in them. If they were to become lawyers, they would win every single argument. They know me, and yet, they try to give me their "research" and their "understanding" of what the Bible says about the topics and struggles they face to benefit them. I take this opportunity to take them deeper into God's Word and, then, to study on that subject. I really love it when they win the argument based on the Word of God, but engineered by me for them, they find answers for themselves.

Parents, it is not easy to parent, especially when living in a time where many are selfish and looking out solely for their own best interest. However, we must apply everything given to us in His Word that the Holy Spirit has taught us and bring it to life for our children to see for themselves.

PRAYER:

Heavenly Father, I ask You to help me parent with the wisdom and understanding that only comes from You. You have given us Your instructions to live by and to teach to our children. Father God, I know You want them to know Your Word and follow Your commands. You have promised blessings to those who walk in obedience to Your Word, and Your Word is powerful to break every selfish desire that our children have.

You have commanded us to teach Your Word and Your ways to our children.

Father God, as Your child, I will obey You and stand on Your promises as these little eyes are watching me. I will let my children see me bow my knee to you, and I will let them see me follow Your written instructions. Help my children to observe and follow You as I am following You.

In Jesus' name, Amen.

THINK ABOUT IT:

What practical ways can you implement discipline for your children in this area?

Write out a prayer, specifically for your children, about this area of discipline.

DAY 8: OBEDIENCE STARTS WITH OBEYING GOD

"If you love me, you will obey my commandments."

— JOHN 14:15

Teaching obedience must start with obeying God, and it is the first thing children need to be taught. That is where it all begins.

We must constantly point to God through our actions and adoration and show our love for God and His Word. Jesus said, *"If you love me, you will obey my commandments."*

We have to teach our children the first greatest commandment, which is to love God with all their heart, with all their soul, with all their mind; we must also teach our children the second greatest commandment, which is to love others as themselves.

Let's start with the first greatest commandment. The word "all" is very significant because it goes before heart, soul, and mind. Notice how God refers to the word "all" over and over again? "All" means entirely and complete and, in essence, perfectly in full.

We should also take notice that God mentions the heart first. Why? Because the heart is evil, and no one can understand it but God. It is also where everything is stored. Therefore, we must teach our children to control their temperaments. The heart is where the feelings are stored, such as love, compassion, affection, concern, pity, sensitivity, sympathy, and understanding, just to name a few.

We teach our children to show tenderness for the hurting. A child's disposition starts with how they respond to those who are hurting; this is why God says to love Him with all our heart. God has this kind of heart. God's temperament is love towards the hurting and the afflicted. Every sentimental feeling, good or bad, comes from the heart. If God is loved there, then our response will be for humanity straight from the heart. Our character, feelings, and nature are birthed from the right kind of heart.

Then, He says, "soul." The soul is our conscience, which is also related to our heart. It is where our intellect comes into play. We must know God, and for us to overcome evil, we must study His Word to become discerning of the attacks of the enemy. Our soul is where our personality and our courage comes from, as well as our attitudes. Our soul is our spirit and who we are flows from our soul.

When you fully study the words "heart," "mind," and "soul," you will find they are all interwoven together. It is where our inspiration comes forth. It is life coming out of us, our secret self, and the breath of life. This is our place of thought and vitality. You can understand why God says we must love Him in this part of our being.

Finally, we must also love Him with all our mind. This means paying attention to His Word, being conscious of who God is. We must bring our vain imagination to a halt with the help of the Holy Spirit, whom God has placed in us.

We must have sound judgment and perception involving all of our senses, our talents, and our functions. Our mentality must be with the power of a sound mind, employing wisdom, knowledge, intellect, and understanding. I could go on and on.

It is imperative for us parents to clearly notice how the three words, "heart," "spirit," and "soul" are woven together. Many of the words I used mean the same for each one. You see why God says "all" before each of them that makes us human? Every fiber of our being is made up of these three things, and He wants us to love Him and others with no compromise and no exceptions.

APPLICATION:

My son, Justin, saw this insight. He said, "Mom, you taught this to us when Ellianna and I were so young."

I love it when my children refer to me teaching them something. He even said, ""Mom, I remember specifically when I was eleven years old, and Ellianna was five years old, and you were teaching this to her." You see, kids do not forget our teachings.

I have certain things that I say repeatedly to my children. "What is in your heart will come forth in your actions." I will not accept anything from them if I detect pretend emotions and not a genuine heartfelt action. I am not being hard on them, just simply showing them what happens when they do something out of obligation; it is felt by the person.

God knows very well the intentions of our hearts. He rejected Cain's offering, King Saul, Ananias, and Sapphira, just to name a few. God knows our hearts. Keeping our hearts pure towards Him is the key. When we teach our children to obey Him first with ALL of their beings, which is made up of their hearts, minds, and souls, then it will come naturally to obey us as parents, teachers, and those in authority. We must train the heart and the mind, and this will raise up children with a soul and a conscience. These are the children who grow up and do great exploits for the kingdom of God and for their generations and those yet to come.

PRAYER:

Heavenly Father, help me to teach my children how crucial it is to honor You.

Help me to train them in the ways they should go, and it begins with obedience towards You. You tell us to obey You with all we have.

I pray that the hearts, minds, and souls of my children are fully bowed down to You and Your ways, Father. How can they obey me or those in authority if they don't first obey You?

I ask for Holy Ghost fire to come upon my children and to have them totally sold out to You. I ask for their "all" to bow before You.

Give them a mind and will to chase hard after You and to obey You no matter what the cost.

In Jesus' name, Amen.

THINK ABOUT IT:

What practical ways can you implement discipline for your children in this area?

Write out a prayer, specifically for your children, about this area of discipline.

DAY 9: CHILDREN MUST RESPECT AUTHORITY

> *"Obey your leaders, and accept their authority. They take care of you because they are responsible for you. Obey them so that they may do this work joyfully and not complain about you. (Causing them to complain would not be to your advantage.)"*
>
> — EPHESIANS 13:17

One of the greatest teachings for our children must be respecting authority. I don't like to skip over or ignore important issues. Unfortunately, this is one of the biggest issues faced by parents in some countries. The Bible is very clear and cannot be made any clearer when it states, *"Obey your leaders, and accept their authority."*

Kids are having a really difficult time understanding and doing this. I am on the side of the kids. If parents don't teach their children about respecting authority, they will do as they think or become influenced by cultural issues which are meant to divide and break. I hear more and more about people name-calling those who are in high authority, law enforcement, and particularly, those whose views are different from their own.

Parents, we must teach our children to show respect. As I have written about in this book, respect means to have reverence, to hold in high esteem, and that we must honor leaders and their authority. It doesn't just say to "obey," it goes on to say, "and accept their authority."

Today's youth do not do any of those things well, and it is absolutely necessary to teach children to use their voices and their voting right against prejudice and injustice.

We do not want to see our children, especially in the household of God, stand before a court judge to be judged and sentenced. Parents, teaching our children to respect the law of the land and those who work to maintain the law is very important. It gives the child the assurance that there are people who care about their well-being. It keeps them secure, knowing there is a protection given to them. It helps them to trust.

Presidents and leaders need to be respected. We respect the office of any leader, and we can teach that we don't like the policies and issues they represent and why they are wrong from a biblical perspective. However, we do not dishonor the office they hold.

Please do not miss this truth: bringing up children to be respectful is going to be in their best interest and to their advantage.

APPLICATION:

In our home, we have a tradition. In September, we take time once a year to visit our local police station and fire station. We go in and bring them trays of food just to say, "Thank you for laying down your lives to protect our lives and our town."

We have done this since my son was two years old. The town knows us, and they have the biggest smiles when they see us walk through their doors.

My son made friends with the chief of the fire department. They told him he could volunteer if he wanted, and when he grew up, he would have a job with them if he chose to. When the fire department goes down our street, they will put on the siren, so my kids know they are saying, "Hello" to them.

We didn't do this to get their attention. We did this to honor, respect, and let them know how appreciative we are of them. We let them know we pray for their safety, and we stand with them. In the process, my son got blessed with a wonderful role model. You see what happens when we teach to "Obey and accept authority"?

I want my children to stand for honor and truth, and I want them to do it with respect and class. They will be the next generation to govern this world by their voices, prayers, and participation as good citizens of the land. God created our children with great purposes and plans to make our world a better place. It starts with "Obeying and accepting our leaders and those in authority."

Remember, Jesus was taken by the soldiers, and Peter took out his sword and cut off a soldier's ear. Jesus rebuked Peter, and then, Jesus took the soldier's ear and healed the soldier. After that, the Christians were martyred and hated. Yet, there was no revolution.

This should teach us how to behave in our world. It is so simple and so clear. Sometimes, I can't write it to make it any clearer. Jesus always shows clearly how we should behave and what we should do. No amount of words can override what He does and says.

PRAYER:

Heavenly Father, we live in a world filled with hatred for authority. Our children are taught to hate those in authority and to blame them for everything; our children are taught to not take responsibility for their behaviors that show disrespect and dishonor. What is worse are their actions against those in authority. Father, I pray that this will not be my children's portion, and I pray You will help them see Your truth.

Lord, with the grace, strength, and help You give me, let me demonstrate obedience and respect for authority to my children. Teach them and help them to learn obedience to leaders and accept their authority.

Lord, You didn't cause a fight when You were led to the cross. Though You were humiliated, mocked, tortured, and finally murdered, You said, *"Forgive them, for they don't know what they are doing."* You didn't defend Yourself, and You had every right. You did everything perfect and good.

I ask You to help me to model an example of obedience to my children.

In Jesus' name, Amen.

THINK ABOUT IT:

What practical ways can you implement discipline for your children in this area?

Write out a prayer, specifically for your children, about this area of discipline.

DAY 10: CHILDREN REAP
WHAT THEY SOW

"He will pay all people back for what they have done."

— ROMANS 2:6

Teaching our children that what they do will come back to them is essential. Sowing and reaping are important life applications. Our actions will come back to either bless or condemn us.

God is very clear in all He does and says. God's Word breaks every chain, every custom, and every tradition that comes against His Word. Every single person will be paid back for what they have done.

We teach our children to always stay true to God and do good deeds. We don't teach them to do good only to some people as long as it benefits them. Instead, we teach our children to be wise with their connections and to invest in people whom God sends their way. We teach them to give to the poor, to help the needy, and to open their hands, throw the bread in the water, and let it swell up even bigger.

We tend to do things for show. God is not impressed with shows. He is impressed by what we do in secret. He loves a heart that gives.

The Word of God speaks about the parable of the landowner leaving the workers an amount of money to invest while he went away. He left money with his workers so they could invest it, and they did it well, except for one. That one who buried the money was afraid of losing it and thought it better to give it back to the master when he returned rather than invest the money and lose it.

Sounds like he did a wise thing, right? He did not. You see, he was lazy and didn't look for opportunities to do what is good. In return, he got nothing. He didn't even put it in the bank to earn interest. Hear what the Spirit is saying to you today. Invest in the lives of your children. Throw all of yourself into raising godly children with everything you have. What you invest will come back to bless you or curse you. God pays back every person for all they have done.

Kids need to understand they have unique talents and abilities given only to them with which to serve God. They are not like anyone else. There's no one like them; no one can take their place. Before God, they have a responsibility to contribute to their world.

No one is created just to breathe air. We have to teach them to get up and do something. We look for their abilities, capabilities, talents, and interests. Then, we push them gently, and sometimes aggressively, towards their calling. When we do this, we build their self-esteem and speak life into their calling. God will bless our children as they move in this way.

Look for your children's giftings and use this verse to show them that God will honor and pay them back for the good they have done.

APPLICATION:

Both my children are givers. I thank God for this. When they were little, I took them to the duck pond. I brought bread with me, and we fed the ducks. As they threw the bread in the water, I remarked about how it swelled up even bigger when they threw it in. I always look for opportunities to bring this truth to the forefront of their minds.

There was one night I can never forget. Justin was seven years old, and this particular night, he refused to do his homework. This was a constant battle (now he is graduated at the top of his high school class, scoring top ten percent in the country in math, science, history, English, and geography), and on this night, out of frustration, I put Justin in the car and drove to Boston, which was a 30-minute drive right into the city.

I found a homeless person. I asked Justin, "Do you want to be like this person? If you don't study and if you don't apply yourself, you will not have a good-paying job."

As we were driving, I found another homeless man, and I pointed to the man and asked Justin, "Do you see that man, Son? That man lost everything. I don't know his story, but is that how you want to live?" My son, in his high-pitched little boy voice, exclaimed, "Mommy, stop the car! We have to give money to him right now and help him."

I was stunned! I began crying to myself, trying to hide the tears from my son as he was sitting in his booster seat in the back. I thought, "God, I tried to teach him something completely different than what he just said. What is this about?" God so clearly showed me that night, "Teresa, I gave your son a heart for the poor and needy, continue to bring him up in My ways. This son of yours is totally Mine!"

I got home and hugged my son. I told him, "Justin, I took you there to show you why you must study, but God showed me your heart. Justin, this is why you must apply yourself. I will help you as your mommy and as your teacher, but those people can't help themselves. So, then, you must study so God can use you to bless them. In your giving, God will always provide for your needs."

My daughter is the same way. Both my kids have more than they can handle, always having to give things away, so many times with tags still on the items. I believe it is because they are givers. However, it is not just about money. It is also about using their talents to bless others.

As I am writing this, my six-year-old niece walked into our office, where Ellianna and I are writing. Yesterday, Ellianna helped her little cousin build a Lego snow house. Her cousin just brought her a Captain America keychain, one of Ellianna's favorite characters. My niece said, "Auntie, I wanted to give something to your daughter because she built something for me, and I want to give something back to bless her."

Angelina, my little niece, is six years old, and she mastered this verse perfectly. Whatever you have to work with, work with it to show your children how God is pleased with a generous heart and will bless them back.

PRAYER:

Heavenly Father, give my children a heart of generosity. Wherever my children go, I ask that they will open their hands and give to those in need. Let them be on the lookout for the ones You bring into their lives that truly need it.

Lord, send my children destiny helpers, and give them wisdom to know the difference between those who would exploit them versus those sent by You.

I ask for You to let them see the principle of reaping and sowing at work in their lives. Let them give double out of their hearts, and when You look at what they have done, You will say of them, "Well done, My good and faithful servants."

In Jesus' name, Amen.

THINK ABOUT IT:

What practical ways can you implement discipline for your children in this area?

Write out a prayer, specifically for your children, about this area of discipline.

DAY 11: LYING IS UNACCEPTABLE

"The faithful few in Israel will not do wrong, tell lies, or use their tongues to deceive others."

— ZEPHANIAH 3:13

L ying is one of my top ten, no-way, unacceptable behaviors. I hate lying. Children who lie will grow up to be disrespected and dishonored. Children are not born liars, but they learn to lie very quickly. This needs to be dealt with immediately. A good character is destroyed with lies. As adults, we all know this.

In this verse, God is speaking about those in Israel. Who are those in Israel? They are His people, us. Therefore, He is saying, *"My faithful few will not do wrong."*

Let's look at this for one moment. We must bring up children who will do no wrong.

Many people say, "We are not perfect." This statement is absolutely a lie from the pit of hell. The Word of God is very clear in the Old and the New Testaments, *"Be perfect as God is perfect."*

This isn't a suggestion. Jesus himself said, *"That is why you must be perfect as your Father in heaven is perfect."* You see, we have no excuse to stand on. We were told to be perfect, and this means we can.

What we can't do is be sinless. We are tempted to sin, but God will make a way in the middle of the temptation to deliver us. Please understand this.

The next thing this verse goes on to say is, " *...use their tongues, to deceive others."* Our tongues have the power of life and death. We kill ourselves and our futures when we condone and excuse lies. We must teach our children this very important truth. No lying under any circumstances.

I understand that in the past, people lied to save people from being killed. Many lives were saved during World War II, hiding the Jews from Hitler's regime. However, little children are not called to save people at an early age. I bring this up because this has been asked of me before. What about the people who saved the Jews during the Holocaust? Of course, I would have lied to save those people, too. However, children are not able to understand this early on, so you teach what is appropriate, and what is appropriate is the Word of God, which tells us we are not to lie.

When they are older, God forbid if there is a war, they will be led by God to do what that hour demands of them. God will give us the words to use when we are instructing what needs to be taught to our children. We don't have to over-think it.

The Spirit of God, who dwells within us, leads us from moment to moment. Lying is very wrong. It destroys good character and the integrity of the person. We teach this early on so they know they are called to a higher standard.

APPLICATION:

Children will push us to see what we will accept and what we will not accept. One of those things they will test is lying. Both my children, when they were young, pushed this button for me, too. Both children tried to lie to me. I had believed them. It was something little, I can't even remember because it was so insignificant, but it was a lie.

Justin and Ellianna were each around five-years-old when they told their first lies. At nighttime, Ellianna came to my room crying hysterically and hyperventilating, and I woke to her crying out, "Mommy, I can't sleep."

"What's wrong?" I asked. "Does something hurt you?" I remember my daughter saying, "My heart hurts, Mommy." I was barely awake and thought, "She can't be having a heart attack." I heard her say, "I lied to you, Mommy, I feel so bad. My heart hurts so much."

I picked her little body up as she sucked her little finger, while tears streamed down her face, and she made those crying moans and groans, and I told her, "Ellianna, God gave you a good heart, and in your heart, there can't be sins of any kind. Your heart is sensitive to the Holy Spirit, and God will never allow you to deceive me and cause you a life of lies and not be trusted by those around you."

We prayed, and she slept next to me in bed that night. When her brother was that age, something similar happened to him. It was like deja vu.

They tried this again as pre-teens; my son, first, since he is older, and my daughter next when she was 12 years old. I remember in both cases I was walking and God told me, "Justin/Ellianna lied. They didn't tell the truth. Go tell them I told you they lied."

I went to them, and I told them, "God just spoke to me. I will ask you once. Either I heard from God or I didn't, so you better answer correctly. God's punishments are not easy like mine. Did you lie?"

As my children were left speechless, the look on their faces told me I heard right from God. There were tears in their eyes, and confession is really good for the soul.

Both children said to me, "Mom, I guess God will not allow me to lie to you ever. Wow, Mom, God really speaks."

I wanted to say, "I told you so!" but I held back. That wasn't a moment to make it about me, but it was a moment for them to learn. I told them, "You better watch your step. God will not be mocked, and God will tell the righteous what is going on behind their back. Be very careful what you do."

We prayed together, and my children have not lied to me again. Each of them lied twice, and that better be the last time. You see, I had already laid out the foundation regarding lying. They watch me, and they know I will not have anything to do with people who lie. They know lying is a terrible character trait, and I will not stand for it in anyone, especially my children. Layout the foundation, and they will follow it. They will test, but they will not get away with it.

PRAYER:

Heavenly Father, Satan is the enemy of our souls, and he is the father of lies. I rebuke the spirit of lying in my children, and I pray you will convict them every time they attempt to lie.

I pray in Jesus' name for the Holy Spirit to come down and not allow them any peace until they confess their wrong and reconcile themselves first to You, and then to me as their parent.

In Jesus' name, Amen.

THINK ABOUT IT:

What practical ways can you implement discipline for your children in this area?

Write out a prayer, specifically for your children, about this area of discipline.

DAY 12: RESPECT MUST BE TAUGHT

*"Honor your father and your mother, so that you may
live for a long time in the land the Lord your God is
giving you."*

— Exodus 20:12

Children do not come preprogrammed with respect, reverence, or consideration to anyone. These are things we as parents teach them. We must teach them diligently because the promised blessing is too enormous to overlook.

God is specific. *"Honor your father and your mother, so that you may live for a long time..."* It really comes to living or dying. This should shake us to our core. We want our children to be blessed with long life. Therefore, let us teach them how to honor us.

The blessing doesn't stop there. It goes on to say, *"live for a long time in the land the Lord your God is giving you."* Did you catch that? God is not just giving you long life, but He also goes on to say He is giving you the land He has promised you. The blessings for this action are way too important to overlook, and God wants us to teach this to our children. They get the blessings of God in the land of the living.

Since honoring your father and mother is one of the Ten Commandments, it is a top priority. What a wonderful promise associated with honor! God sees this as very sacred, and we must also take it seriously and make it first priority.

APPLICATION:

My children have been taught to show respect by watching very carefully what they say to me. In other words, no disrespectful word is to ever leave their mouths towards me.

When they were little, I explained the importance of them keeping watch over what they said about us parents. That meant they were not to use curse words or swears toward us; they were not to speak words of hate when they disagreed with us.

When they said something wrong, they were punished by going to their rooms and having their toys taken away. I followed them into their rooms and explained this verse. Then, I asked them to sit there and think about what they did, telling them to pray and ask God if I was wrong, and if I was wrong to give me a Bible verse to back it up.

I knew God was not going to condone them fighting or not listening to what I had to say, but it brought them to a realization of the wrong they committed and it brought them to God. At some point, they had to admit they were wrong and apologize. I still carry this to this day, and I tell them, "Show me where I have wronged you, and I will retract the punishment."

PRAYER:

Heavenly Father, I honor You with my life, and I want my precious children to live for You, for them to receive the inheritance and reward You have for them.

Help me to teach this important commandment to my children because I want to see my children live a long and prosperous life and receive all the gifts You have for them, and their future, and generations to come.

I rebuke now the Devourer who comes to steal, to kill, and to destroy their inheritance and their rewards. In Jesus' name, Amen.

THINK ABOUT IT:

What practical ways can you implement discipline for your children in this area?

Write out a prayer, specifically for your children, about this area of discipline.

DAY 13: HONORING PARENTS IS HONORING OTHERS

"Honor your father and your mother as the Lord your God has commanded you. Then you will live for a long time, and things will go well for you in the land the Lord your God is giving you."

— DEUTERONOMY 5:16-18

E very single day, we demonstrate to our children how to show honor. Honor is important to God, and it is one of the Ten Commandments.

We must show our children that it is a privilege to honor their God and their parents, as well as those who they come in contact with. Honor will merit them respect, recognition, and distinction amongst the rest.

When children are taught to respect others, it is credited to the children. The children will gain admiration from those who are watching and receiving the honor due them. There is an essence of great pride and joy by both the giver and the receiver.

People take notice when they see anyone showing honor to others, especially when it is children who are showcasing it. In a world where there is such disorder and dishonor, we are to teach what the Word of God says about honor. It starts in the home with children honoring their parents. This command comes with a blessing.

We must show our children the importance of honoring God, you as the parents, and all others they come in contact with.

APPLICATION:

Since my children were young, I modeled the behavior of honor towards their grandparents and others. I also took them shopping to pick a small gift for me for Mother's Day and their father for Father's Day, birthdays, and Christmas. It wasn't because I wanted their gift. It was because they were being taught the importance of remembering, not only by their words, but also by action.

When they were small, I would choose a chocolate bar and then share the chocolate with them. This showed the blessing immediately. This was instilling in them a very important principle. Honor brings distinction amongst the rest, and honor brings blessings.

As teenagers, my children, on their own, began taking me shopping and honored me by buying gifts for me, and the result of this has caused them to experience blessings.

PRAYER:

Heavenly Father, true wisdom comes from You alone. Your Word says to ask for wisdom because You give wisdom generously to all who ask.

Lord, I come before You today asking for Your help. In accordance with Your Word, help me to teach my children how to honor You first and us second.

To You, honor is so important that it is in the Ten Commandments. Honor is not optional, but it is a must for my children to receive blessings.

This world is filled with chaos, selfishness, and dishonor. I come against these things in the name of Jesus Christ, and I proclaim my children will honor You first. Honoring You first is where it all begins.

Father, I pray for the grace and the patience to show my children honor, too. You remind me not to cause my children to stumble and fall. Let the Spirit of the living God enlighten my mind as to how to teach this to them and keep my children from bringing dishonor to You and us.

Lord, I know you have them in the palms of Your hands. Lead me to teach and model Your Word very well to them.

In Jesus' name, Amen.

THINK ABOUT IT:

What practical ways can you implement discipline for your children in this area?

Write out a prayer, specifically for your children, about this area of discipline.

DAY 14: CHILDREN ARE OUR CROWNS

"Grandchildren are the crown of grandparents, and parents are the glory of their children."

— PROVERBS 17:6

This Bible verse is all about honor. I spoke about honor being the "crown" in the book's introduction, and I said we wear our children as a treasure on our crown.

When we bring up respectable and honorable children, it affects not only us, the parents, but also their grandparents. You, as their parent, are rewarded, and their grandparents are also rewarded.

Look at what the second part of this verse says, *"Parents are the glory of their children."* You see something interesting here? All of a sudden, we, the parents, are mentioned as being their glory. This happens when we teach and bring up children of great character.

This job surely isn't for the faint of heart. Parenting takes a lot of hard work and sometimes much pain. However, parenting can be done with the help of God.

We need the wisdom and guidance of the Holy Spirit to show us how to parent. I love that it says, *"Parents are the glory of their children."* So, then, what does this mean? It means we will be recognized for parenting well. We receive all the praise and can claim the fame and prestige that comes with this tough job, the grand finale, which I love so very much.

It's like God says, "Teach them honor and you will receive the honor!" Wow, God! I love these moments when God shows me something so great. Start teaching honor, and you will receive the honor, too.

Teach honor to your children, and honor will come back to you. This gift is reserved for parents and children. Thank You, God!

APPLICATION:

My children, Justin and Ellianna, went to the bank with my parents on a weekly basis. When the Vice President and the rest of the employees found out they were my children, they told me, "Wow, you are the mother of Justin and Ellianna? Your children are absolutely awesome. It is a pleasure to see them come here. They are so polite. It is impressive how they act. They bring you honor. You are an incredible mother."

They brought me glory. I taught my children to honor those who serve them, even if they don't know the people.

I taught them to acknowledge our fire department and police station, visiting them and bringing them food. This teaches them to honor those to whom honor is due.

We don't show honor to be admired. We do so because we are to honor not just parents, family, friends, and co-workers, we must teach them to honor those they don't know, and those who work behind the scenes, too.

PRAYER:

Heavenly Father, help me demonstrate to my children how to respect and honor those around us through my words and actions.

Help my children to honor You, our family, those they come in contact with, and those they deliberately seek out.

Help my children to be the light of this world in the dark places. Father, let their light shine by honoring others.

Let them rejoice and delight themselves in You and in what You have called them to do in this world for those in their generation.

Give them a heart that bows before You so they do what You expect them to do.

Lord God, let their boast be in You alone.

Father, I ask that You let them bring in beauty where there are ashes, and I ask that You use my children for Your glory.

In Jesus' name, Amen.

THINK ABOUT IT:

What practical ways can you implement discipline for your children in this area?

Write out a prayer, specifically for your children, about this area of discipline.

DAY 15: SELF-ESTEEM
ACCORDING TO GOD'S WORD

"I can do everything through Christ who strengthens me."

— PHILIPPIANS 4:13

B uilding self-esteem in children is very important and must be done early when they are babies. Children are like sponges. They take in every word spoken by us and others. What we say to them is what they believe they are.

As godly parents, we build self-esteem according to the Word of God. We look for things they are particularly good at and praise them. This encourages them to have self-esteem. We look at things that are weaknesses in them, and we work towards strengthening those things.

We must teach them that their identity is in Jesus Christ. Once they realize their identity in Him, they can conquer the negative messages when they come their way.

We teach them how to have confidence in their own abilities, teaching them that God created them to be them. No one can accomplish what they were called to accomplish. They are uniquely designed to make a huge impact in this world.

We have to help children understand that they were created with great purposes. Satan always tries to destroy what God has created. It starts with children feeling they are worthless. We break that lie in Jesus' name by pointing to scripture and helping them understand they walk with God, the One who gave them their life.

It starts with teaching them self-respect. Once they learn how to respect themselves, then they begin to take pride in themselves. Healthy pride is important and necessary. They must hold themselves up to their own dignity, have faith in themselves, and they must have self-confidence in who they have been made to be by the Great Master Potter, God.

The best thing you can do for your child's self-esteem is to point them to God and show them their identity in Him.

APPLICATION:

My son, Justin, struggled with math but was absolutely brilliant with history, geography, and English. I first concentrated on how brilliant he was in certain subjects. I picked things out, like his ability to remember details of who was who in history. I purposely got myself lost while driving so I could ask him for help with how to get home. I knew where I was, but I wanted him to use his knowledge of geography. So, I led him to believe I was lost and needed him to get us home. Then, I made a huge deal about how smart he was in geography.

When it was time for math, I told him, "Justin, math is like learning another language. You speak English and Italian. Now you have to learn how to speak math." For every math problem he could solve, I clapped and shouted, "Wooooooo-Hooooo! You see? You can do it, Justin."

He finished math with an A! Was it difficult and painful? Yes, but he learned he could do everything through Christ, Who gave him the strength to do it.

PRAYER:

Heavenly Father, You are the One Who gives us worth, and because of that, I pray that You specifically help me teach my children that they can do anything through You. Apart from You, O God, we cannot do anything, but with You, we can do all things.

Help me to teach them Your ways. You promise in Your Word that you have plans for good for them, not disaster, and those plans will give them a future and a hope.

Lord God, show them how You define them, what their identity is in You, and that in You, they are giants and made victorious.

In Jesus' name, Amen.

THINK ABOUT IT

What practical ways can you implement discipline for your children in this area?

Write out a prayer, specifically for your children, about this area of discipline.

DAY 16: CHILDREN ARE A ROYAL PRIESTHOOD

"However, you are chosen people, a royal priesthood, a holy nation, people who belong to God. You were chosen to tell about the excellent qualities of God, who called you out of darkness into his marvelous light."

— 1 PETER 2:9

This verse holds a special place in my heart. Everything we need to teach to our children about who they are in God is found right here in this passage. Let's look at it together.

When teaching self-esteem, the child must know their identity is in God. God is clear. They are a royal priesthood. By definition alone, it is part of a royal family, meaning king and queen. They need to see their identity as to who they are in accordance with the Word of God.

They are above all the things that try to tear and bring them down. Sometimes, people try to bring us down.

Bullying in school has become a major problem. I taught my kids never to allow anyone to bring them down to their level of evil and never to be malicious. Peers try to tear us down with their unkind words and actions.

As an educator, I have written much about self-esteem and those who try to belittle us, especially in the school building. However, I taught my children they are a royal priesthood. They do not bow down to anyone who will try to intimidate them by their evil actions.

Our children are a holy nation. This is why Satan uses people to attack our children. If we explain it is the spirit within them who attacks us and not the people themselves, they will have a different mindset. They already won.

Our children belong to God. They were chosen to tell about the excellent qualities of God. Therefore, they are not in darkness and already know about the attacks which will come their way. They walk in God's marvelous light. They are extraordinary, incredible, and awesome creations.

APPLICATION:

Ellianna never wanted to learn a second language. I speak Italian fluently and so do many family members. She just didn't want to learn.

I knew what was in her. I know she needed me to build her up. She didn't think she could do it. She not only learned to speak Italian, but she also realized she wanted to learn other languages!

She came to me to tell me she signed herself up to learn how to speak French and wants to learn how to speak

Romanian. I don't know why Romanian, not my first choice, but I'm going with it. You understand my point here?

How does a child, who doesn't want to learn to speak a language, do a complete turnaround to learn Italian, work on French, and now want to add another language that's not as popular? I told her she could do this, and I told her she would rock it. I told her I had faith in her to learn how to speak Italian. You see how self-esteem is so powerful?

PRAYER:

Heavenly Father, You are the One who gives us our worth because You have chosen us and identified us as Your own. Please let me parent well by listening to You and by being led by Your Holy Spirit.

Father, help me to build my children's self-esteem by understanding my identity in You so that I am able to teach it to them.

Help me to see with the eyes of the Spirit what You have made my children to be.

Lord God, let me not be deceived by any negative things my kids may say. Instead, I ask you to help me see them the way You see them, and please help me to assist my children in seeing all the purposes and plans You have created for them, and then give me the power to help them realize their identity in You.

In Jesus' name, Amen.

THINK ABOUT IT:

What practical ways can you implement discipline for your children in this area?

Write out a prayer, specifically for your children, about this area of discipline.

DAY 17: CHILDREN WERE NOT GIVEN THE SPIRIT OF FEAR

"God didn't give us a cowardly spirit but a spirit of power, love, and good judgment."

— 2 TIMOTHY 1:7

As we conclude on this subject, I can't express enough how important helping our children have a good and healthy self-esteem is to them and their future decisions. Kids grow up believing they can't do things.

We have looked at the previous Bible verses that teach us who we are in Him. Therefore, a fearful spirit must be broken.

The following Bible verse says the kind of spirit He didn't give us and the kind of spirit He put down deep in our hearts. It is those things that we must instill in our children. We help them understand and discover what is deep inside of them.

God says, *"I did not give you a cowardly spirit."* This means we teach our children to not be afraid. They aren't running away from things because they think they can't do it. Instead, God has given us a spirit of power, love, and good judgment.

We must teach our children to love who God made them to be, and every single gift they have must be explored. For example, my daughter is a born writer. She has been writing since she was four years old.

We must teach our children to love who they are. This is so important. As a youth leader, I came across many kids who didn't like themselves. I am a self-esteem builder, and I went out of my way to look for the ones who didn't love themselves and then showed them how to love themselves by seeing themselves as Jesus sees them.

Please, parents, teach your children to love themselves by the way you love them. Encourage them, and build them up. Don't tear them down.

Finally, we must teach our children to use good judgment in everything they do. There is so much I want to write about just based on the Spirit of power, love, and good judgment. Please write these down, and allow the Holy Spirit to lead you in teaching them to your children.

APPLICATION:

When Ellianna was five years old, she said, "Mommy, what are you doing?" I said, "I am writing a book." She said, "Ok, Mommy. I want to write a book too." Immediately, I told her, "Ok, here is your notebook. Sit here next to me, and you write too."

The look on her face is still engraved in my mind forever. She was my thumb-sucking child. She removed her finger from her mouth, and she sat next to me with her little notebook and pen and wrote the most amazing little devotional ever.

My friend loved it and published her devotional on a Facebook fan page. Over 25,000 people loved it and shared it. That was the beginning of Elliana's writing. She had discovered a talent she had and her self-esteem soared. It was a moment in history for her and me.

PRAYER:

Heavenly Father, You are the One Who Gives Understanding, and today, as I am here praying for my children, I ask You to help me understand the Spirit of power, love, and good judgment.

My desire is for my children to be filled with Your power and Your love. I ask that You, O God, fill them with good judgment. Let my children put on the mind of Christ so they may bring glory and honor to You.

In Jesus' name, Amen.

THINK ABOUT IT:

What practical ways can you implement discipline for your children in this area?

Write out a prayer, specifically for your children, about this area of discipline.

DAY 18: THEIR BODIES BELONG TO GOD

"Don't you know that your body is a temple that belongs to the Holy Spirit? The Holy Spirit, whom you received from God, lives in you. You don't belong to yourselves. You were bought for a price. So, bring glory to God in the way you use your body."

— 1 CORINTHIANS 6:19-20

We live in a world where our children are taught their bodies belong to them. This is not scriptural at all. If we, as parents, do not understand this truth, we are in trouble.

We must use the Word of God to debunk all the evil thoughts and ideas our precious children are taught. We fight evil by arming ourselves with the most powerful thing, the Sword of God, which is His Word. God's Word is our weapon of warfare.

Let's look at the first verse above. God is asking a question. Just like we ask our children questions that we know they know the answer to already, God is clearly saying we are not our own. Our body is the temple of the Holy Spirit. He lives in us. We need to teach our children that the way we use our bodies must bring glory to God. We must teach this truth immediately.

We can tell our children their bodies are wonderfully made, and their bodies belong to God. He wants our bodies to be healthy in mind, spirit, soul, and body. As soon as they understand sex, and that depends on the child, we begin to talk about purity. We need to help them understand sex is a beautiful thing, created by God, and their body is to be shown only to the person they marry on the marriage night.

If we talk about sex from God's perspective, our children will understand. We should not be ashamed about sex. We need to present it as something good and pleasurable, not dirty and shameful. For our children to have a healthy view of sex, we need to address sex from God's perspective. So we start off with this verse, which is clear and precise.

APPLICATION:

When my children were little, I talked to them about their bodies being beautiful. They were created with their own uniqueness. I pointed to their eyes and their hair and make remarks about their color, their noses, the shape of faces, etc. I told them their bodies had the Holy Spirit in them, and Jesus lived in their hearts.

Then it was easy when they got to the age of under-standing for them to relate to the fact their bodies belonged to God, and they couldn't just give it to anyone. It had to be a person they loved deeply and were married too.

I explained another verse found in 1 Corinthians 6:12, which states, *"Someone may say, 'I'm allowed to do anything,' but not everything is helpful. I'm allowed to do anything, but I won't allow anything to gain control over my life.'"* I explained to them that they had to exercise self-discipline, which means they can't put themselves at risk.

Sex outside of marriage is sinful, wrong, will hurt them, and will hurt God.

PRAYER:

Heavenly Father, You are the God Who protects, and I ask You to keep my children safe from all harm. In a world where promiscuity is accepted and celebrated, open the eyes of my children to see the truth.

Lord, let them hear Your voice whisper in their ear the truth about sex.

Keep them pure and give them an undivided heart to prevail against a generation that is doing things to hurt themselves and defile their bodies.

Help them to see their bodies are a gift given to them by You, and let them know they are the temple of the Holy Spirit.

Give my children a conviction to keep their sexual purity for their future spouse.

Give them the courage to stand for truth and to bring honor and glory to You in the way they use their bodies.

In Jesus' name, Amen.

THINK ABOUT IT:

What practical ways can you implement discipline for your children in this area?

Write out a prayer, specifically for your children, about this area of discipline.

DAY 19: UNDERSTANDING SEXUAL PURITY

> *"It is God's will that you keep away from sexual sin as a mark of your devotion to him. Each of you should know that finding a husband or wife for yourself is to be done in a holy and honorable way, not in the passionate, lustful way of people who don't know God."*

> — 1 Thessalonians 4:3-5

Parents have the authority given to us by God Himself to help our children understand sexual purity.

He has given us Scripture to back up everything we say. I always address my children with, "The Word of God says. It is not me but God's Word. Do you want to know what God thinks and has to say?" God is very clear. We are people who know Him. Therefore, we must act in a holy and honorable way.

God has a will, and His will is that we keep away from sexual sin. This is the only sin where we sin against our bodies and against God. It is a double whammy.

Our bodies are the temple of the Spirit of the Living God, which means our body is not our own but belongs to God. When we give in to sexual sin, we join our bodies with someone else's body, which is also a temple. When our body joins with another, there is a spiritual connection that takes place.

Children need to know God is not a killjoy. He created sex for our enjoyment within the boundaries of marriage between a man and a woman.

We need to explain that we open ourselves up to another person when we have sex. This means we are uniting ourselves with the person. So, it is not just a one-night stand. Our heart, soul, mind, and body are opened to them. We become one with each other. This is the outcome of sex.

We need to explain in today's age, there are diseases spread through sex that are deadly. Our one-night stand with someone who isn't ready to commit or who is playing the field can lead us to a life of illnesses. What's worse is they can die from AIDS or other sexually transmitted diseases.

Contraceptives can fail, and a young woman can become pregnant. Then there are choices to make, such as adoption or keeping the baby. For a believer, abortion is murder. We cannot cut short the life of a human because we have messed up. We cannot be afraid of telling the truth here.

Parents, at times, we forget what it was like to be a teenager with raging hormones, and we all know what happens with teenagers with raging hormones. As parents, we are responsible before God to teach what is right, not just teach it but guard and lead our children to make good choices.

Don't encourage dating when you know the hormones of teenagers are all over the place. You can't expect a child to date and not kiss. When there is a kiss, hormones rage. We have voluntary and involuntary muscles. Involuntary muscles are activated, and then people can't stop. Need I say more?

APPLICATION:

I have a rule. I brought my children up with the rule of no dating until they are ready to commit to marriage. Then, they are to date according to the teachings of the Bible. Go out with a bunch of friends but no coupling up.

My kids understand this truth. It didn't just come to them. I taught it, and I continue to stand my ground.

They understand God's Word, and they want to honor God. As a parent and as a youth leader, I found kids want to do what is right. But the "right thing" needs to be lovingly explained and demonstrated to help them live up to the expectations.

I tell my kids, "God did not make rules we can't keep." He knows we can; it's a choice.

What will your choice be?"

PRAYER:

Heavenly Father, help my children honor You in all they do and help me teach my children about sexual purity. Their bodies are the temple of the Holy Spirit, and I ask You to make known to my children how important it is to maintain their purity until their wedding night.

Keep them sexually pure, and help them to understand what the Word says about purity.

I ask that You open their minds and make known to them what is right and holy before You. Keep their minds steadfast on what You desire.

In Jesus' name, Amen.

THINK ABOUT IT:

What practical ways can you implement discipline for your children in this area?

Write out a prayer, specifically for your children, about this area of discipline.

DAY 20: PURITY IS ONE OF OUR MOST VALUED POSSESSIONS

"Let marriage be held in honor among all, and let the marriage bed be undefiled, for God will judge the sexually immoral and adulterous."

— HEBREWS 13:4

Our children need to understand why purity is one of the greatest things we possess. This passage helps them understand this truth. This is Truth 101. Our children must be taught marriage is something we are to honor.

Our bodies don't belong to us only. They belong to the person we marry too. God honors marriage, and marriage is holy. Godly marriages are a gift we offer God. We cannot defile the marriage bed. God will judge the sexually immoral people and the adulterous people.

Please understand God is saying two things. The sexually immoral are all those who commit sexual sins. The adulterous people are the ones who are married but cheat on their spouses. God is covering the sexual sins of both in one passage.

Since we want to build excellent moral standards for our children, we must be clear in what we say to them and what God has to say.

I do not allow movies or books in our home that go against the Word of God. We, as parents, are responsible for whatever we allow our children to watch and read. One of the most important things we can teach our children is to be loyal, faithful to God, themselves, and their future spouses.

APPLICATION:

The best way for me to explain this is through this story.

When my son, Justin, turned 16 years old, one of the gifts I gave him was a purity ring for his future wife. I took him to the jewelry store, and I told him to pick whatever ring he wanted to present to his wife on their wedding night.

My son told the jeweler what he was doing. Everyone stopped to hear him. They were shocked by what he had to say. I saw a few grins of pride from people and a few smug faces, but I didn't care. I knew God was pleased by what He saw.

Justin picked a ruby ring. He said, "Mom, I am picking a ruby ring because the Bible talks about finding a wife that is like a ruby. I want a ruby kind of wife, Mom, so I picked a ruby to give to my wife on our wedding night."

I will never forget the scene and never forget his look of determination and pride on his face.

He wears this ring on a gold chain around his neck and above his heart, signifying his commitment and faithfulness to a young woman he has yet to meet. His body is for her, along with his heart, love, mind, and every fiber of who he is. I suggest this is something you do with your child too.

PRAYER:

Heavenly Father, You are the God Who watches over us. I ask You to keep my children pure and to give them hearts to do what is right.

Give them the will to pursue righteousness and to seek after You all the days of their lives.

Keep my child away from temptation and under the shelter of Your wings.

Keep a hedge of protection around my children, and let Your grace be their covering.

Let them look only to You, O God, and keep them from the lies of the adulterous one who will try to seduce them.

My children's bodies belong to You. Father, for their future spouse, I ask for You to keep their spouse pure and holy before You.

In Jesus' name, Amen.

THINK ABOUT IT:

What practical ways can you implement discipline for your children in this area?

Write out a prayer, specifically for your children, about this area of discipline.

DAY 21: BODY IMAGE IS IMPORTANT

*"I will give thanks to you because I have been so
    amazingly and miraculously made. Your works are
    miraculous, and my soul is fully aware of this."*

— PSALMS 139:14

B ody image is a huge issue in our society. For those who are raising daughters, we must be cautious about how they perceive themselves. This is so important.

I have raised both my son and my daughter to make healthy eating choices and to thank God for their bodies because it is God who formed them.

I remind them God took particular care in creating them. They have to take care of their bodies now. Most importantly, I speak to them and tell them how good they look.

I help them choose foods that are good for them. We make decisions together about what we will eat, involving them in the food purchase and preparations. It might sound silly, but my kids read back labels to see what's in the product. They know those fancy words for fake stuff, and they automatically put it back on the shelf. If I should purchase something by accident, I have to return it because, after they finish reading the ingredients, they determine for themselves whether an item is not healthy.

However, this Bible verse is much more important. Here, the psalmist was praising God and thanking God for creating him. You see, it says, *"I will give thanks."* We must teach our children to appreciate their bodies. We are to recognize what God has done. The psalmist says, *"My soul is fully aware of this."* We help them to be well informed that God created a masterpiece in them. He made their eyes and hair and chose the colors of them, and He chose their body shape as He saw best for them.

God created them with great care, so they need to take care of their bodies. They do this not for sex appeal, but because God didn't create them to be filled with diseases.

Boys want to be all muscles, and sometimes, they get involved with steroids, which will harm their bodies. Girls are vulnerable to anorexia and peer pressure from media ads. We must combat these harmful worldly ideas and thoughts with the truth from the Word of God.

APPLICATION:

I homeschool my children. Therefore, I teach health and gym. Justin picked running. We had to exercise 4 times a week and run less than 40 minutes (3 miles). Can I just admit it was challenging?

We learned we love to do this, and we continue to exercise together. These moments are precious. We discuss things during our run. It has brought us closer together and has given us a tighter relationship. I get to hear his heart, his dreams, his plans, and what is inside of him. I have these moments to encourage and get him to think even more.

With Ellianna, at age 10, she was 5 feet tall. She is super tall. She had a problem with this because every kid was half her size, and every boy was way shorter than she was.

I had to do a lot of encouraging. She complained a lot. She saw herself as different, and the truth is she was. The clothes she had to wear were tailored for a 16-year old. She struggled with her body. I spoke the above verse over her every single day. I added, "Ellianna, you have the body of a model, and someday, you will be grateful. Don't be upset. God knew what He was doing when He created you. There is a reason for your height. Thank God for making you so special and unique."

You see, as parents, we don't pretend what they are seeing is wrong because that is worse. Rather, we look at them, build up what needs to be built up, and incorporate what needs to be incorporated to help them.

If your child is a little on the heavy side, don't call them fat. That is horrible. Rather, set them up for success by what you teach them about food and exercise.

In our household, we eat food that helps us stay healthy and strong, and we have a bit of junk food such as cookies, ice cream, and cake. I teach exercise is important to build strong bones and keep our minds alive and active.

I read studies on good nutrition and exercises with my children. The important thing is that we teach the whole approach for spirit, mind, body, and soul. We do it God's way, not the world's way.

Daniel and his friends chose the right foods to eat, and the Bible says they were healthier and brighter than those who ate the rich foods. We have plenty of examples to work with.

PRAYER:

Heavenly Father, reveal Yourself to my children as You have revealed Yourself to me.

Reveal to them who they are in You.

Guard them against the ideas of this world, which may cause them to do things to their bodies that will harm them.

Lord, let them see they were created beautifully in Your image. Let them make wise choices for their bodies to keep them healthy and disease-free.

In Jesus' name, Amen.

THINK ABOUT IT:

What practical ways can you implement discipline for your children in this area?

Write out a prayer, specifically for your children, about this area of discipline.

DAY 22: DEALING WITH FEAR

"Even when I am afraid, I still trust you."

— Psalms 53:6

Right from the beginning, children will tell us they are afraid of the dark, sleeping alone, etc.

Some fear is a good thing. For example, I strongly feel no matter who the person is, if the child isn't comfortable with that person, do not leave the child alone with that person. The person might be great, or they might not be. Don't push your child. Watch the situation and see where it goes from there.

It is perfectly all right for the child to feel afraid in certain situations. It's an emotion God has placed within us, like a warning, such as don't jump in front of a car or approach a wild animal to play.

However, there is the wrong kind of fear, such as fear of the unknown, fear of going to school, or they may be irrationally fearful of other things.

We need to tell our children that fear is something God created to help us not make mistakes that will hurt us, and give them examples, like playing with matches, substance abuse, or disobeying and getting punished. Having a fear of the Lord is a good fear.

Irrational fears or phobias are not good. Children will wake up with nightmares and then want to sleep with you. These moments are important teaching opportunities. We take the child, wrap our arms around them, making the child feel safe, and then, we talk about God.

This Bible verse is an easy one to share and help kids remember what the Word says: *"Even when I am afraid, I will trust you."*

Kids need to know that it's normal to be afraid to a certain degree, and in place of fear, they need to know God will not abandon them. They can trust Him to help them when fear comes.

We teach faith in God Who will not fail us. We can have confidence in Him, Who will deliver us from all evil. We can place our hope in Him and be assured beyond any doubt God will be with them. Our children don't have to be anxious about anything. With God, we overcome all our fears.

APPLICATION:

Both my kids dealt with fear. As children, they were afraid of the dark. They were afraid to sleep alone. So, I would lie down with them until they fell asleep. Then, I would go into my room.

Sometimes they woke up and came to my bedside, saying, "Mommy, I am afraid. I want to sleep with you." I would get up and go and lie down with them. Then, they would fall asleep, and I would leave when I knew they were sleeping comfortably.

During those times, I told them, "God has His angels all around your bedroom," and then I said, "God will not allow any harm to come to you. Tomorrow morning you will tell me if God failed you." Of course, God never failed them. I knew I was teaching them they could trust God and fear not.

When my children became teenagers they dealt with some health issues. Both my children were frightened, as was I.

I will never forget God dealing with me. "Step out of the way," he told me. "How are your children, that I placed into your hands, ever going to know Me and who I am, if I don't allow the testing to come to them? I will heal them. Let me do what I need to do in their lives. They must have their own faith, trust, and belief in Me, not rely on your faith."

It was painful to see my kids sick, but God was faithful, especially with my son. Once a week, for months on end, we had to get blood work, and Justin hates blood work and was fearful of that needle. I talked him through, and I held his hand while they drew his blood. "Justin, fear not, God is with you. There is no fear with God. He will deliver us a good report."

We stood on God's Word. God was faithful, even if on the inside I was panicking. My son only heard, "Justin, I am not afraid, and neither should you be. God is with you, and God has healed you."

As parents, we need to speak life into our children. We boldly proclaim, *"If God is with us, who can be against us? What can man do to us?"* And we need to learn to be truthful and remind them, we can feel afraid, but it is an emotion, "Even when I feel afraid, I will still trust in God."

PRAYER:

Heavenly Father, thank You for the healthy fear that You have placed in our hearts.

Thank You for the fear which makes me do what is right in Your eyes, and shun what is evil , and I pray that this kind of good fear be a constant companion to my children. Your Word says, *"The fear of the Lord is the beginning of wisdom."* Let my children fear You, O Lord, and honor You always.

Let any phobia or fear that comes to their mind be broken in the name of Jesus.

Use all the scary situations to remind them they can trust You to deliver them from all their troubles.

God, You never fail. In the darkest times, You shine the greatest and brightest. Father, help my children to learn this secret weapon for deliverance.

Lord, help me to demonstrate to them how to use Your Word to fight fear, and help them learn to use Your Word to combat and break through their fears.

In Jesus' name, Amen.

THINK ABOUT IT:

What practical ways can you implement discipline for your children in this area?

Write out a prayer, specifically for your children, about this area of discipline.

DAY 23: DEALING WITH PREJUDICE

"God corrects you as a father corrects his children. All children are disciplined by their fathers."

— HEBREWS 12: 7

As parents, we have a responsibility to teach our children, *"God made everyone in His image."* This means we love and respect everyone regardless of their skin color, religious beliefs, or nationality.

Prejudice is among the most destructive things on Earth. It breeds hate and attitudes of supremacy. We must eradicate and bring down all prejudice. Hate for others is bred from a lack of respect for other people, their looks, their customs, and their beliefs.

God is the God of love, and He says, *"Love others as you love yourself."* Period! It does not say, "Love those who believe like you, look like you, and act like you."

Children, by nature, accept everyone. Notice how they love everyone when they are babies and toddlers?

Something happens when they begin to get a little older. We begin to see signs of not liking other children. They don't play nice in the playground. As they get older, in their pre-teen and teen years, it gets worse. All of a sudden, they make fun of other kids.

Let's think about this for a moment. How could this have happened? It's a very easy question to answer. It is called learned behavior. They have learned from the behaviors of others. They learn from other family members, their peers, and through social media peer pressures. Because we are their parents, we need to break those lies, behaviors, and actions.

We must teach them God's truth. We bring God's Word into their lives, so they are not deceived by the evil and ungodly ways of the world. We explain we came from one man; his name was Adam. From there, God made every single nation.

He is God the Creator. He made humanity, and then, He spread them all over this earth; each person wonderfully and beautifully made in His image. When we tear someone down with our words, we are slapping God in His face. We are saying, "You created something unpleasant," when He says, in Psalms 139:14, *"I will praise Him, for I am fearfully and wonderfully made."*

When we begin to teach our children that it is God who made all of us different and that we are all fearfully and wonderfully made, prejudice is eradicated.

APPLICATION:

I have friends from all over the world, and my children automatically, from birth, accepted everyone.

However, I had a role to play also. Since they were little, my role was constantly introducing them to different cultures and different ways of doing life. I only spoke about how God expects us to live and act. So, then, the color of someone's skin or other traits that look different from them never played a negative role.

My application to my children was the Word of God. We have a standard to live by in our home that is measured by what the Bible has to say. We respect people and their beliefs. We don't have to agree with their beliefs if it is contrary to the Word of God. It is fine. Our job is to be godly and love others.

Talking about the beautiful places and all the richness that has been brought forth from other cultures is important to us and our world. God is very clear, He made everyone.

I remember telling my children about Moses and his wife, who was black. I told them how his sister Miriam wasn't happy that Moses married a black woman. God brought His judgment on Miriam, and she became a leper. Moses had to pray for her to be healed.

God is not going to bless those who make fun of His precious children because they are different.

PRAYER:

Heavenly Father, You are the God of all love and justice. We are living in a world of hate, filled with prejudice. Protect my children against this evil that divides and breeds hate and intolerance towards others and their ways.

Lord, please keep my children from committing this evil against You.

Help them to build bridges of love, not hate.

Help them to showcase Your love for others and appreciate them for who they are.

Let my children be known as vessels of love and respect for humanity.

Father, let them never compromise the living Word of God within themselves, and let them be the shining light in this dark and hateful world. May they always proclaim and point to you, the Savior of all humanity. Where there is hate, let love brightly shine so those around them can see You in them.

Let them bring peace through the lives they live in honor to You.

In Jesus' name, Amen.

THINK ABOUT IT:

What practical ways can you implement discipline for your children in this area?

Write out a prayer, specifically for your children, about this area of discipline.

DAY 24: AVOIDING UNHEALTHY FRIENDSHIPS

"Friends can destroy one another, but a loving friend can stick closer than family."

— Proverbs 18:24

As parents, we are to be very careful who we allow our children to play with. Friendships are necessary, and important, but the wrong friendship can lead your child astray. I have seen many children turn from God and all His ways because parents were not careful in supervising their children's friendships.

It is perfectly normal for parents to carefully watch the ones their children hang around with. Let's take a good look at this verse. *"Friends can destroy one another."* I'm not willing to have my children destroyed by another person. My kids know the importance of making and keeping good, godly friendships.

Friends can fail us. We need to help our children know there is one friend who will never fail them. His name is Jesus. He is our friend for life. He will always stick by us no matter what. At the same time, we can help our children pray and ask God to bring them godly friends who will speak truth and wisdom into their life and they, in turn, can speak truth and wisdom into their friends' lives. Friendships are an important part of life. Friends are there to encourage us and help us.

However, there is only one friend who will stick closer than family, and that friend is Jesus. When children know there is a friend who will never fail them, there is a security within themselves that they can count on Jesus.

This is what we want to do as parents. We want to showcase Jesus as their personal Savior, Master, and Lord of their lives, and someone that is trustworthy and dependable when life struggles are too much to bear. No human person can ever take the place of Jesus.

At the same time, we teach our children to be loyal and faithful to their friends, but they are never to lie, never to cover up lies, and never to conceal wrong behavior. Teach them not to participate in any wrongdoings; it is perfectly fine to walk away from bad behaviors of friends who will bring dishonor to them.

Teaching children to say "NO" to their peers is important. They don't have to do things that bring them shame and embarrassment to be a friend to someone or do things that they know are sinful or make them feel uncomfortable. Many times, children are afraid to tell their parents what is going on. Please listen: never make your child feel they can't tell you what is happening with their friends.

Friends build up and support each other. They encourage and rejoice with each other's successes. They do not bring down, threaten, and destroy.

APPLICATION:

I have been very strict in this area. I have told my children, "No, I do not like the behavior of that child, and I will not allow you to hang out with them." Do not be afraid of saying this to your children.

My daughter has a best friend, and thank God, it is her cousin, my brother's daughter. I can trust my daughter with her just as I trust my brother and my sister-in-law. I am so glad God gave her a good and godly friend.

My daughter wanted a best friend. We prayed about this, and God had her best friend in the family. I share this to say God honors us when we pray about everything, including friendships for our children.

My son has his three uncles, and they are his best friends. I know there is an age difference, but honestly, it is not that much. It is humbling to see my son talk to his three uncles about everything and to see the relationship they have. I am blessed that God has honored my children's desires to have good godly influences of friendships.

My son will call his uncles to hang out with him. Just last week, he told me, "Mom, I am going to go out with Uncle Joe, and have a cup of coffee with him, Ok?" He came back home and went running with me. In the run, he told me how they spoke about God's Word and how they had a great time talking about trucks and other things men talk about. I thanked God in my head. God sent my kids friendships that are meaningful and protected them from all harm. How blessed are my children!

Your children can and will also be blessed. Don't push just to have anyone as a friend; not all friends are good things. Be selective, and be wise in making friends. Today's society is not the same as when you and I grew up. Not all houses are safe, and you, as the parents, must be wise to protect your child.

PRAYER:

Heavenly Father, You are the God who cares about relationships, and I know You want us to have good and godly friends. Lord, I do not know the hearts of men, but You look to the heart and not the outer appearance.

Please bring my children friends who are godly and will influence my children in the ways of the Lord. Let my children respond in kind.

Let the relationships my children have be pleasing in Your sight. Most importantly, teach my children that You are the one Friend Who sticks closer than a brother, Who will never leave them nor forsake them.

In Jesus' name, Amen.

THINK ABOUT IT:

What practical ways can you implement discipline for your children in this area?

Write out a prayer, specifically for your children, about this area of discipline.

DAY 25: HYPOCRISY DESTROYS

"Whoever says, "I love God," but hates another believer is a liar. People who don't love other believers, whom they have seen, can't love God, whom they have not seen."

— 1 JOHN 4:20

Hypocrisy is deception because it is pretending to be something you are not. To pretend to be something you are not is deceitful and dangerous. We have a soul and a conscience, and the only people we are deceiving is ourselves. Children pick up on what we do, and then they imitate us.

One terrible hypocrisy is the way we pretend to love others. God is clear on this. In fact, God is very clear in all He says and does. God isn't sugarcoating anything. When we pretend to love others but really hate them, God says,

"You are a liar." Ouch! We are breaking one of the Ten Commandments, "Do not lie."

Parents, I caution you. Please be very careful how you deal with hypocrisy. I am just covering one of the ways here. I chose this verse because we are all guilty of this. We get mad at people for actions they have committed against us or perhaps even causing pain.

Satan is a liar, and he comes to steal and destroy what belongs to God. He never wins if we choose to live by God's Word. Hypocrisy is a terrible thief. It steals our character, integrity, honor, and genuineness.

Everything we teach our children is all about living a life of godliness. Hypocrisy is the total opposite. It is an act. The word "hypocrisy" is derived from the Greek word meaning "Actor. A person who is wearing a mask." What an actor does is pretend to be someone he or she is not. God calls it hypocrisy, and He calls hypocrisy a sin.

Basically, what hypocritical people do is to profess belief in something, and then act in a manner contrary to that belief. We are God's holy people. We walk with integrity, character, and honor. We must choose to live our lives in righteousness and reflect God in all we do.

God does not lie, and God never pretends. He speaks truth, and we must teach our children to do the same.

APPLICATION:

For my children, this has been a part of their everyday life. When they are disappointed in someone or something, they will privately go to that person. They will tell them, "I love you, and you mean much to me, so please can I share my honest feelings with you?" Taking this position has been a blessing.

There is so much deception and dishonesty all around us and in our world. We need to raise up children who can speak truth in love and be wise when they share their feelings and thoughts and when they can't.

There are times they can't share with the person because that person isn't ready for the truth. In those cases, they know to just watch carefully what comes out of their mouths so they can't be accused of saying things they don't mean.

God says, *"He makes a way of escape for us."* I believe this means in everything that pertains to us, who are His children. God never allows us to compromise, and He always gives us the correct words to speak in any situation. We do our children an injustice when we do not teach them this truth. For every single situation they find themselves in, God is with them. He delivers them from their troubles. It is all about wisdom in how they approach the situation.

Teach children to pray and to ask God for wisdom. God said, *"Let the children come to me."* Therefore, we teach our children in the toughest of situations to go to Him, and He will guide them into all truth.

PRAYER:

Heavenly Father, this world is filled with pretense, deception, and hypocrisy, even in the church. Help me showcase truth, honor, integrity, and character. Let me shine forth Your truth.

Father, please instill these traits in my children as I am instructing them in Your ways. Help them to see You in all things.

Help them to have an open heart before You. Help them to be honest children who stand out from among those in their generation.

You, O Lord, are the Light of the World, and let them shine as a beacon of light in the darkest of places.

Let Your light radiate and show them they can trust You completely.

Be their guiding Light when they are in the darkest places and lead them through those places. Let them be a light shining brightly to everyone around them. In Jesus' name, Amen.

THINK ABOUT IT:

What practical ways can you implement discipline for your children in this area?

Write out a prayer, specifically for your children, about this area of discipline.

DAY 26: LIFE IS SACRED

"I was placed in your care from birth. From my mother's womb you have been my God."

— Psalm 22:10

Today, our society has no value for the sanctity of life. Sanctity of life means "holiness of life and character," and it also means "godliness, the quality or state of being sacred." I find it interesting that the word "holy" is mentioned 431 times in the bible, and if you include the words "holiest," "hallowed," and "holiness," it is used over 500 times. God is trying to tell us something. I feel led by the Spirit to cover this topic. I know it is difficult, but we cannot sugarcoat things for our children because the world is filled with sin and deception.

In this day and age, children go to school intending to kill their schoolmates and many times succeed.

Children are told they can do whatever feels right for them and do whatever they wish with their bodies; that means they can have sex. If the girl gets pregnant, she has a right to her body to get an abortion.

This is not what the Word of God has to say on the subject. Right from the start, in the beginning, in Genesis 1:27, it states, *"So God created humans in his image. In the image of God, he created them. He created them male and female."* There are 21 references in the Bible from Old Testament to New Testament, repeating God created man and woman in His image. In Genesis 9:6, it states, *"Whoever sheds human blood, by humans his blood will be shed, because, in the image of God, God made humans."* You see why we must be very clear with our children about this truth?

God never looks the other way when we sin. There are consequences to our sins, and there are consequences when we disobey the laws of the land too.

One major lie of the enemy has come in the form of abortion. We must teach our children to do what is right in the eyes of God. God is the Giver of Life. He gives a birth date and a death date. It is all written in His book. When we teach truth to our children, the Holy Spirit takes over and shows them the truth. We cannot avoid this topic because we must help our children understand it. God placed every person as a baby in the mother's womb.

From the very beginning, we were in His care. He has been our God right from the start, from in our mother's womb as told to us in Psalms 139:13: *"You alone created my inner being. You knitted me together inside my mother,"* with another 11 cross-reference verses, repeating the same thing. We cannot skip over this or take this lightly.

Our children must know the truth and stand on the truth. It doesn't matter what the world teaches or what their friends think. We bring up our children upon the Word of God. This is what we have to stand on, and this is what they have to stand on.

Be wise. Don't skip over important topics or feel ashamed to discuss them. There is nothing we, as parents, can't discuss with our children. We are their most important teachers.

APPLICATION:

My children clearly understand they are to respect and celebrate life. I'm going to get personal because this is a crucial topic, and must be addressed in a godly manner. Sometimes, we break the isolation people feel by discussing the issues from a biblical perspective.

My children have been vaccinated against all diseases. My son and daughter were offered a vaccine to prevent a certain type of cancer spread by sexual acts. My son told the pediatrician, "I am a Christian, and I will not be engaging in any sexual activities. I am waiting for my wedding night." I don't think I could have been prouder than when I heard him say this to his pediatrician. He was of age to make up his own mind about the vaccine. I know my son is very serious about this.

Next came my daughter. Since she was not at an age for her to make up her own mind, it was my choice to allow it or not. In the presence of my daughter, her doctor, and a student doctor, I openly talked about our position and the consequences of sex outside of marriage. I said, "In our home, my children have been taught early on about the sanctity of life. We have discussed contracting diseases by having sex outside of marriage, which can lead to death and abortion. In our home, abortion is not an option, which means my children, especially my daughter, would have a choice to make. Keep the baby, or put the baby up for adoption, or have an abortion. We know abortion kills the life of a human being. Therefore, my children fully understand the consequences of sex outside of marriage and the results of it."

Ellianna picked up where I ended and told her pediatrician, "My values are for life. I will not be compromising myself for any kind of sexual acts because I don't believe in acting that way. I want to honor God with my body."

If ever I was proud, it was at that moment. You see, my children didn't come up with those answers on their own. They needed to be taught sex is something really beautiful and amazing, but outside of marriage, it becomes ugly and unfulfilling, causing sicknesses and diseases, and worse, they would be jeopardizing and risking their lives. You might get pregnant, and then you are faced with abortion, which could lead to murdering a human life.

Don't be afraid to speak to your children on issues that will be life or death to them. Our job is to teach, teach, teach, teach, and then teach. We also teach by what we do. The best teaching is done by actions.

PRAYER:

Heavenly Father, we live in a wicked world where what is honorable and true is no longer the case.

Father, many are calling good evil and evil good. What is evil has replaced what is righteous.

In Jesus' name, I ask for wisdom to teach my children what is right in Your eyes.

Lord, give me the words to help them see they belong to You and that You see life as sacred and something to be honored. You expect us to protect life.

Father, let my children love the people around them and view every life that comes before them as sacred and holy before You.

Father, protect them from evil and let Your will be done on Earth as it is in Heaven concerning every aspect of their lives.

Let them see that You placed them in my womb.

Help them see and understand You are their God first and foremost.

Lord, let them see the importance and value of life, and protect my children from the lies of the enemy.

Keep them safe from all harm.

In Jesus' name, Amen.

THINK ABOUT IT:

What practical ways can you implement discipline for your children in this area?

Write out a prayer, specifically for your children, about this area of discipline.

DAY 27: COMPASSION

"Speak for them and be a righteous judge. Protect the rights of the poor and needy."

— PROVERBS 31:9

C hildren need to know how much they have been blessed. The blessings come from our heavenly Father, who gives us good and perfect gifts.

We are to share and give to God and others while protecting the rights of the poor and needy. This is at the core of Jesus' heart. He had compassion for the poor and hurting.

Greed is always a problem in our hearts. Have you ever watched little children play in a group, and suddenly another child comes along and takes away the toy the other child was playing with? You see the shocked little face, and then that child goes and tries to take it back. Well, this is a common factor in every person's life.

We must teach our children sensitivity to the needs of others. We are to teach them to care for the poor and the needy and to show concern for those who can't help themselves. We are to teach them to have mercy towards those who are less fortunate. Charity is one of the greatest gifts. As the Word of God says, *"If we don't have love, we have nothing."* Therefore, teaching how to love others as we love ourselves is vital to the child learning sympathy.

It doesn't cost anything to show kindness. In this verse, God tells us to protect the rights of the poor and needy. It isn't a suggestion of what to do for them, but instead, it is a command. We are to speak, be a righteous judge, and protect them. The ones who are the greatest are those who have done unto the least of them.

APPLICATION:

It was Christmas time, and we were putting a Christmas gift into a shoebox to be given out to the poor. Justin was about five-years-old. I took him to the store to pick what he thought were good gifts to add. I explained we needed to give shoes, clothes, candy, and toys. We picked everything up, took it home, and began to place our items in the box.

I wanted Justin to participate for himself. So, I asked him, "Justin, is there something special that you want to give to this boy?" He collected little racing cars. He had lots of them. Justin took the cars he was playing with and held them tightly in his clenched hand, bringing his hand to his heart with that look in his eyes.

"Mommy, no way. I am not going to give him anything that belongs to me."

I said, "Ok, Justin, no worries. I thought maybe you had in your heart to give something too." He walked away, thinking, while I was praying, "God, please give Justin a heart of compassion and love."

A few minutes later, he came back with one little car in his hands and said, "Mommy, I want to give the little boy my favorite race car," as he handed me his most beloved race car.

At first, I tried to give it back to him and told him to choose another race car less meaningful. God spoke to me, "Let him give what I placed in his heart to give. Do not take this away from him."

I said, "Ok, Justin. You go ahead and place it in the box." I wanted him to feel it for himself, placing the gift in the box. We drove the box to the church as they were about to ship it off.

Justin never forgot that moment, but it was the first step in having a heart for missions. Justin is a giver, and it started when we put together the Christmas box, and Justin decided to give what was in his heart to give.

PRAYER:

Heavenly Father, You are the God of compassion, and Your compassion is unfailing.

Father, give my children a heart of compassion and develop within them a spirit of sensitivity towards those who are poor and in need.

Let them feel genuine concern for those who are hurting. Let them show love, kindness, and mercy.

Give them tender hearts and let them be sympathetic towards others and to go beyond sympathy and be empathetic. Empathy will change their hearts to do what is good for others.

Give them a great love for the poor, and use their lives to become blessings in this hurting world.

In Jesus' name, Amen.

THINK ABOUT IT:

What practical ways can you implement discipline for your children in this area?

Write out a prayer, specifically for your children, about this area of discipline.

DAY 28: GENEROSITY

"Besides, God will give you his constantly overflowing kindness. Then, when you always have everything you need, you can do more and more good things."

— 2 Corinthians 9:8

God is generous. He is the Giver of our very life, and He gives our heart's desires. He gives our daily bread. He is always giving and gives us beyond what we could ever ask or think.

No wonder He wants us to give also. In this verse, we find God gives and provides us with all we need so we can do more and more good things.

Children, by nature, are selfish. We need to continually help them see that a selfish spirit is not blessed by God. When we open our hands with hearts of gratitude and give back, His kindness and the blessings flow.

We don't give to get back; we give because we understand that God will bless us in our giving. Because He is generous, we imitate him, and we must be generous too. God promises we will always have everything we need.

As we teach this beautiful Bible truth, remember the three principles:

1.We give because God gives us constant, overflowing kindness.

2.We will have everything we need for our daily lives and sometimes beyond what we need.

3.We give because we can do more and more good things for the kingdom of God.

APPLICATION:

It was Saturday night. Justin was ten-years-old, and he received a birthday gift of 100 dollars. We went to church, and it was missions Sunday. At the end of the service, the ushers stood by the door to receive the offering for missions.

Unbeknownst to me, Justin took out his wallet and pulled out his 100 dollar bill and put it in the bucket.

I am sorry to say that I was upset because it was his birthday money, and he had already said what he was going to purchase. I knew he would then ask me for the money.

In the car, I said, "Justin, why did you give all the money? Now, don't ask me to give you the money, and now you will not have the money to purchase what you need."

It was not a proud moment for me, friends. Justin's answer shocked me. "Don't worry, Mommy, I felt God tell me to give it all, so I did. I will not ask you to give me any money."

We drove directly to my parents' house for our normal Sunday lunch. As soon as we entered my parents' house, my Dad said, "Justin, I'm so happy to see you. Go get my wallet, please."

Justin went to get the wallet, my dad opened it and handed Justin a 100 dollar bill! Justin's face lit up like a Christmas tree. "Mommy," with that little boy's pitched voice, "look! God gave me back the 100 dollars. You see, Mommy? I will have the money to get what I want, and the missionaries will have the money to get what they want, too."

Friends, I am so ashamed of myself even writing this here. How dare I do what I did! God taught me a lesson that day, and I never forgot it.

When it comes to our children, we allow them to give what it is in their hearts to give. God rewards accordingly.

PRAYER:

Heavenly Father, You are the Giver of all that we have. We can never out-give you. Please help me to teach this vital lesson to my children.

You, O God, love a cheerful giver, and You love when we show love and compassion to the poor.

Please uproot all selfishness from my children. Help them to see that when they give all, You will give back *pressed down, shaken together, and running over*.

You give more than they can hold and more than they could ever use. Lord, bless my children so they can become a blessing to others who are in need.

In Jesus' name, Amen.

THINK ABOUT IT:

What practical ways can you implement discipline for your children in this area?

Write out a prayer, specifically for your children, about this area of discipline.

DAY 29: TITHING

"Bring the full amount of your tithes to the Temple, so that there will be plenty of food there. Put me to the test and you will see that I will open the windows of heaven and pour out on you in abundance all kinds of good things."

— MALACHI 3:10

Tithing teaches children to give back to God what belongs to Him. God considers us as thieves when we do not give Him what belongs to Him.

God doesn't want to take from us. Instead, He is trying to teach us something, the importance of giving. He already owns everything in this world, including our lives. Our lives are gifts to us, to bring us joy, and to bring him honor. It is the principle of the matter.

I talked about honoring our parents on Day 13. As parents, we teach children to give us gifts, not because we want to take from them but because of their honor, respect, and appreciation towards us. It is in the same idea, and it is a way we teach our children to give to God what belongs to God. It is their way of being grateful and thankful for all God has given and done for them in their lives. God always gives it back to us. This principle is imperative to teach our children.

In my home, my children must tithe from everything. They tithe money they earn from chores, money received as gifts, birthday gifts, Christmas gifts, etc. They are required to give ten percent to God, and they get to keep a little for themselves, but the rest goes into their savings accounts. It is something they do automatically.

Because my kids see how blessed they are, they give their ten percent plus an additional offering to God. It is amazing how God provides for them abundantly.

My son's entire tuition for school, his entire school career, was paid for in full. My daughter took courses outside what is required for her schooling. She loves animals, and her extra studies were paid for in full. She learned about animals at Busch Gardens and SeaWorld. She took every class possible in those places.

I know it is because of God's blessings in their lives. You see, we don't teach just to teach. The lessons we teach are very important, and they are godly principles that will determine their blessings throughout their lifetime.

APPLICATION:

It was the Summer of 2012. Ellianna was 7 years old. We had vacation Bible school, and they were collecting money for missions. The last night Ellianna took all her piggy banks, all filled with money, and she told me she was going to give to the missionaries.

I guess I didn't learn my lesson from my son and his 100 dollars. I told her, "Ellianna, you are going to give it all away? Why don't you just give one of the piggy banks?" She insisted.

I still remember her little blond curly hair flying outside the door of the church while her little hands were carrying a bag with all her piggy banks. She walked to the registration table, took each of her piggy banks, and emptied out all the money she had. There were plenty of dollar bills. Her grandparents and aunts and uncles always contributed to her piggy banks, and they always gave large bills.

I was thinking to myself, "Oh, God, now she is going to ask me for money," but I didn't say anything. I remembered Justin's lesson.

That night, after VBS, she was crying. I asked her, "What's wrong?" She told me that a girl had received a bike that night, and she wished she had a bike. I told her, "Ellianna, your birthday is coming up soon. I will buy a bike for your birthday."

However, as I was driving, God said, "Go to the store now and get her a bike." It was almost 9 p.m., and I didn't want to rush to get her a bike, so I went to the closest store near me.

When I got there, she picked her bike, and, of course, it was top of the line. My children have expensive taste. When I went to place the order, the guy told me they were sold out of the bike she had chosen. It would take two weeks for it to come in.

Ellianna started to cry, not taking a fit, just tears streaming down her face. The man saw her, and I was in front of her. I never saw her crying. He said, "I just put this bike together this morning. I want your daughter to have this bike. I will not charge you for assembly, and I'll give you 50% off, plus, I don't know why, but I feel compelled to give you an additional discount, and I will throw in whatever accessories you want, Ellianna."

I couldn't believe what I was hearing. Still, I knew God was taking over and teaching my daughter He was blessing her for what she had just given two hours earlier to missions at church. My daughter received a $300 gift, and I paid 29 dollars. We still talked about that bike six years later.

Dear parents, we can never out-give God. Teaching to give to God what belongs to Him brings blessings.

PRAYER:

Heavenly Father, all good and perfect gifts come from above. My children are gifts given to me by You, and Lord, I am giving them back to You. They are Yours already.

Help me to teach them that it is better to give than to receive. The joy of giving is satisfying and brings joy to those who are hurting and need our help.

Father, I ask You to help my children give first fruits to You, and help them give out of generosity and love.

Let them show compassion even if they have to go without.

Provide our daily bread for our children, and grant them the desires of their hearts only to bring You glory.

In Jesus' name, Amen.

THINK ABOUT IT:

What practical ways can you implement discipline for your children in this area?

Write out a prayer, specifically for your children, about this area of discipline.

DAY 30: BLESSINGS AND CURSES

> *"Carefully obey the Lord your God, and faithfully follow all his commands that I'm giving you today. If you do, the Lord your God will place you high above all the other nations in the world...*
>
> *Obey the Lord your God, and faithfully follow all his commands and laws that I am giving you today. If you don't, all these curses will come to you and stay close to you."*
>
> — DEUTERONOMY 28:1, 15

Anyone who is acting as a child's parent or guardian must understand Deuteronomy 28. Please hear me. The Word of God, from Genesis to Revelation, holds treasures of blessings for God's children.

In today's society, our children are taught they can do anything because God is a God of love. That is a lie straight from the pit of hell.

Our children cannot be deceived by believing they can do whatever they want because God will forgive them and give them multiple chances. Absolutely a lie from Satan. God will always forgive us when we truly repent, but we will pay the consequences of those sins.

Throughout this book, I have pointed out this biblical truth through the Word of God. Even though this last devotional will be longer than the rest, I have been told by the Holy Spirit to include Deuteronomy 28 because if this isn't followed, nothing I have spoken about will work.

You must sit down with your children and read these blessings and curses together. Help them clearly see what their inheritance is in Jesus Christ. God always comes to the rescue when they call upon Him in the day of trouble. He bends His ear and hears their cry. He moves the clouds and reaches them. He pulls them out of the miry clay. These promises are for His real children. I am going to just list the Bible verses.

Blessings

> *These are all the blessings that will come to you and stay close to you because you obey the Lord your God:*
> *You will be blessed in the city and blessed in the country.*
> *You will be blessed. You will have children. Your land will have crops. Your animals will have offspring. Your cattle will have calves, and your flocks will have lambs and kids.*
> *The grain you harvest and the bread you bake will be blessed.*

You will be blessed when you come and blessed when
    you go.
The Lord will defeat your enemies when they attack you.
    They will attack you from one direction but run away
    from you in seven directions.
The Lord will bless your barns and everything you do.
    The Lord your God will bless you in the land that he
    is giving you.
You will be the Lord's holy people, as he promised you
    with an oath. He will do this if you obey the
    commands of the Lord your God and follow his
    directions. Then all the people in the world will see
    that you are the Lord's people, and they will be afraid
    of you. The Lord will give you plenty of blessings:
    You will have many children. Your animals will have
    many offspring. Your soil will produce many crops in
    the land the Lord will give you, as he swore to your
    ancestors.
The Lord will open the heavens, his rich storehouse, for
    you. He will send rain on your land at the right time
    and bless everything you do. You will be able to make
    loans to many nations but won't need to borrow from
    any. The Lord will make you the head, not the tail.
    You will always be at the top, never at the bottom, if
    you faithfully obey the commands of the Lord your
    God that I am giving you today. Do everything I'm
    commanding you today. Never worship other gods or
    serve them.

— Deuteronomy 28:2-14

Curses

> Obey the LORD your God, and faithfully follow all his
> commands and laws that I am giving you today. If
> you don't, all these curses will come to you and stay
> close to you:
> You will be cursed in the city and cursed in the country.
> The grain you harvest and the bread you bake will be
> cursed.
> You will be cursed. You will have few children. Your land
> will have few crops. Your cattle will be cursed with
> few calves, and your flocks will have few lambs and
> kids.
> You will be cursed when you come and cursed when
> you go.
> The LORD will send you curses, panic, and frustration in
> everything you do until you're destroyed and quickly
> disappear for the evil you will do by abandoning the
> LORD. The LORD will send one plague after another
> on you until he wipes you out of the land you're
> about to enter and take possession of. The LORD will
> strike you with disease, fever, and inflammation; heat
> waves· drought, scorching winds, and ruined crops.
> They will pursue you until you die. The sky above
> will look like bronze, and the ground below will be as
> hard as iron. The LORD will send dust storms and
> sandstorms on you from the sky until you're
> destroyed.
> The LORD will let your enemies defeat you. You will
> attack them from one direction but run away from
> them in seven directions. You will become a thing of

horror to all the kingdoms in the world. Your dead bodies will be food for all the birds and wild animals. There will be no one to scare them away. The LORD will strike you with the same boils that plagued the Egyptians. He will strike you with hemorrhoids, sores[j] and itching that won't go away. The LORD will strike you with madness, blindness, and panic. You will grope in broad daylight as blind people grope in their blindness. You won't be successful in anything you do. As long as you live, you will be oppressed and robbed with no one to rescue you.

You will be engaged to a woman, but another man will have sex with her. You will build a house, but you won't live in it. You will plant a vineyard, but you won't enjoy the grapes. Your ox will be butchered as you watch, but you won't eat any of its meat. You will watch as your donkey is stolen from you, but you'll never get it back. Your flock will be given to your enemies, and no one will rescue it. You will watch with your own eyes as your sons and daughters are given to another nation. You will strain your eyes looking for them all day long, but there will be nothing you can do. People you never knew will eat what your land and your hard work have produced. As long as you live, you will know nothing but oppression and abuse. The things you see will drive you mad. The LORD will afflict your knees and legs with severe boils that can't be cured. The boils will cover your whole body from the soles of your feet to the top of your head.

The LORD will lead you and the king you choose to a nation that you and your ancestors never knew. There

you will worship gods made of wood and stone. You
will become a thing of horror. All the nations where
the LORD will send you will make an example of you
and ridicule you.

You will plant many crops in your fields, but harvest
little because locusts will destroy your crops. You will
plant vineyards and take care of them, but you won't
drink any wine or gather any grapes, because worms
will eat them. You will have olive trees everywhere in
your country but no olive oil to rub on your skin,
because the olives will fall off the trees. You will have
sons and daughters, but you won't be able to keep
them because they will be taken as prisoners of war.
Crickets will swarm all over your trees and the crops
in your fields.

The standard of living for the foreigners who live among
you will rise higher and higher, while your standard
of living will sink lower and lower. They will be able
to make loans to you, but you won't be able to make
loans to them. They will be the head, and you will be
the tail.

All these curses will come to you. They will pursue you
and stay close to you until you're destroyed, because
you didn't obey the LORD your God or follow his
commands and laws, which I'm giving you. These
curses will be a sign and an amazing thing to warn
you and your descendants forever. You didn't serve
the LORD your God with a joyful and happy heart
when you had so much. So you will serve your
enemies, whom the LORD will send against you. You
will serve them even though you are already hungry,
thirsty, naked, and in need of everything. The LORD

will put a heavy burden of hard work on you until he destroys you.

The LORD will bring against you a nation from far away, from the ends of the earth. The nation will swoop down on you like an eagle. It will be a nation whose language you won't understand. Its people will be fierce-looking. They will show no respect for the old and no pity for the young. They'll eat the offspring of your animals and the crops from your fields until you're destroyed. They'll leave you no grain, no new wine, no olive oil, no calves from your herds, and no lambs or kids from your flocks. They'll continue to do this until they've completely ruined you. They will blockade all your cities until the high, fortified walls in which you trust come down everywhere in your land. They'll blockade all the cities everywhere in the land that the LORD your God is giving you.

Because of the hardships your enemies will make you suffer during the blockade, you will eat the flesh of your own children, the sons and daughters, whom the LORD your God has given you. Even the most tender and sensitive man among you will become stingy toward his brother, the wife he loves, and the children he still has left. He will give none of them any of the flesh of his children that he is eating. It will be all that he has left, because of the hardships your enemies will make you suffer during the blockade of all your cities. The most tender and sensitive woman among you—so sensitive and tender that she wouldn't even step on an ant—will become stingy toward the husband she loves or toward her own son or daughter. She won't share with them the afterbirth from her body and the children she gives birth to. She will secretly eat them out of dire necessity, because of the hardships your enemies will make you suffer during the blockade of your cities.

You might not faithfully obey every word of the teachings that are written in this book. You might not fear this glorious and awe-inspiring name: the LORD your God. If so, the LORD will strike you and your descendants with unimaginable plagues. They will be terrible and continuing plagues and severe and lingering diseases. He will again bring all the diseases of Egypt that you dreaded, and they will cling to you. The LORD will also bring you every kind of sickness and plague not written in this Book of Teachings. They will continue until you're dead. At one time you were as numerous as the stars in the sky. But only a few of you will be left, because you didn't obey the LORD your God. At one time the LORD was more than glad to make you prosperous and numerous. Now the LORD will be more than glad to destroy you and wipe you out. You will be torn out of the land you're about to enter and take possession of.

Then the LORD will scatter you among all the people of the world, from one end of the earth to the other. There you will serve gods made of wood and stone that neither you nor your ancestors ever knew. Among those nations you will find no peace, no place to call your own. There the LORD will give you an unsettled mind, failing eyesight, and despair. Your life will always be hanging by a thread. You will live in terror day and night. You will never feel sure of your life. In the morning you'll say, "If only it were evening!" And in the evening you'll say, "If only it were morning!" You'll talk this way because of the things that will terrify you and because of the things you'll see. The LORD will bring you back to Egypt in ships on a journey that I said you would never take again. There you will try to sell yourselves as slaves to your enemies, but no one will buy you.

— DEUTERONOMY 28:15-68

APPLICATION:

There is nothing for me to explain. The blessings and the curses are clearly defined. From the moment my children could comprehend, I broke the blessings and curses down into an age-appropriate level for them.

We always concentrated on the blessings and I spoke a little bit about the curses when they were little. Every time they did something in obedience to God or towards me, I commented, "Get ready! God is going to bless you!" Surely God will bless them in a way that they understood.

Let me tell you my children challenged me too, and there were times when those curses had to be brought out because they did something that caused consequences. They would get their Bible (or now the phone) as they looked up those Bible verses. I only had one question: "What did God tell you in His Word that would happen for obedience or disobedience?"

When they did things that were not according to the Word of God, their little faces went into a look of horror. I allowed them to experience that horrible feeling. It was the best thing I could have done. Coddling them for doing wrong is setting them up for a false sense of security. My children always came back to me crying and whimpering, and we prayed together that God forgave what they did. It was nothing major, but it was just a teaching moment for them to understand that had it been something dramatic, their consequences would have been worse.

We underestimate children's understanding. They know more than what you think.

My children know that all of the promises in the Bible, from Genesis to Revelation, are for them. All they have to do is put into practice Deuteronomy 28.

I want to thank the Lord, and I praise His name for the wisdom He has given to me as their mother as I sought God on my knees. This is what we must do as parents.

Righteous children are not just born that way. It is the responsibility of parents to teach a child biblical truths that will sustain them for life. Proverbs 22:6(KJV) says, *"Train up a child in the way he should go: and when he is old, he will not depart from it."* Did you see that? That is a command, not a suggestion. When God entrusts you with the lives of your children, you are to raise them in the ways of God. This is what this book is all about. You do it with integrity. You do it with love. You do it without fear. You set the bar of excellence for your children. Your children do not set the bar for you. You teach biblical truths unashamed and without holding back.

What you sow is what you reap, and we want to reap one generation after another of men and women of God.

PRAYER:

Heavenly Father, You are the Shepherd of our hearts and the Guardian of our souls. You alone are to be worshipped and praised.

Above You, there is no other.

Let us discipline our children always with integrity and honor, especially now that we have concluded this study on parenting.

Give us the wisdom to raise our children in Your ways.

Let us be models of doing Your will as our children follow in our footsteps.

Remind us that if we want our children to grow up to be warriors for You, this requires us to pour Your Word into their lives, set the example for them, to bless them, and to pray the Word over their lives.

Help us to never take the responsibility we have as parents lightly. Let us be able to parent our children as You parent us.

Give us the strength and the endurance we need to teach them Your love as well as Your anger.

Teach our children You are the One who sets the standard of holiness, and they are responsible before You for every single choice they make, every word they speak, and every action they take.

Flood them with the power of Your Holy Spirit and give them a determination to live for You in these days. Give us as their parents the knowledge and wisdom in every aspect of parenting.

Guide us and be our Instructor in all things.

In Jesus' name, Amen.

THINK ABOUT IT:

What practical ways can you implement discipline for your children in this area?

Write out a prayer, specifically for your children, about this area of discipline.

PUTTING ON THE ARMOR
CONCLUSION

"For this reason, take up all the armor that God supplies.
Then you will be able to take a stand during these evil
days. Once you have overcome all obstacles, you will
be able to stand your ground. So then, take your
stand! Fasten truth around your waist like a belt. Put
on God's approval as your breastplate. Put on your
shoes so that you are ready to spread the Good News
that gives peace. In addition to all these, take the
Christian faith as your shield. With it you can put out
all the flaming arrows of the evil one. Also take
salvation as your helmet and the word of God as the
sword that the Spirit supplies. Pray in the Spirit in
every situation. Use every kind of prayer and request
there is. For the same reason, be alert. Use every kind
of effort and make every kind of request for all of
God's people."

— EPHESIANS 6:13-18

I want to close with this very powerful passage. It must be taught early to our children.

I find it interesting that this chapter begins with addressing the children, *"Children, obey your parents because you are Christians. This is the right thing to do. Honor your father and mother that everything may go well for you, and you may have a long life on earth."* This is an important commandment with a promise.

I have already addressed these verses in the previous pages of this book. There is a reason why it is mentioned in the same passage as putting on the armor of God. It is all about children understanding these truths we have been studying in this book this month.

Children are like sponges; we must fill their lives with the constant truths of God's Word. The world lies, and the world is filled with sins. Someone is teaching your child their voices. Do you have a voice to speak into their lives? A voice that reminds them of God's love, and God's hate for sin? God's blessings instead of God's curses?

The very next verse says, *"Fathers, don't make your children bitter about life. Instead, bring them up in Christian discipline and instruction."* Do you see these truths here? We are not to bring up children who are bitter in life. How does that happen? It happens when they don't know truth. We are commanded to bring up our children in Christian discipline and instruction. We must incorporate the two.

We discipline by helping them obey God's laws, follow His living Word because it has the power to bless them, and give them a hope and a future. We are their authority, and we are their leaders.

We don't rule with an iron fist. We gently guide them into all truth. Praying always for them. Explaining why we put on the armor of God and how to put it on.

God is the God of order. It is important to show them what each piece does and what it means for them to be "geared up." The truth is that Satan is relentless in trying to destroy and bring down Christians. Teaching them how to dress is very important. When they are little, we tell them why we put on their clothes. The clothes represent protection from the elements. You put on a coat when it is cold to keep you from frost bite and a rain coat when it is raining to keep you from getting wet and keep you dry. We use a helmet when we ride our bikes to protect our head against a concussion.

All of these things are important. Let's look at each one more carefully.

Taking Up the Armor of God

For this reason, take up all the armor that God supplies. We start with helping them understand they are given all the necessary equipment to make them win and conquer the war. God is their Supplier of everything in every situation. They can stand securely during evil days. They will overcome all their obstacles.

Just like a soldier puts on his gear, our children must put on their spiritual gear. If you are a soldier, you have to be on the offensive and the defensive. To defend yourself, you have your weapons, and then you have to be on the offensive, meaning you have to aggressively attack the enemy when the enemy is coming at you.

Satan is our enemy, and we're not fighting against flesh and blood. For this very reason, we suit up with the full armor of God; you are gearing up. Do not underestimate Satan. The equipment you have is from God alone to come against the enemy when the enemy comes at you. This must be taught to your children, and you must pray over your children.

You must teach them how to put on the armor of God just like you teach them how to put their clothes on in the morning. In other words, you tell them just as they put on their clothes in the morning, they need to stop, and they need to pray, putting on each piece of the armor.

They need to pray each of the pieces of the spiritual armor over them.

The Belt of Truth

Fasten truth around your waist like a belt because the belt holds up everything. Truth is what conquers everything. If we teach truth, then it will hold them up in every area of their lives.

The truth will set them free. It is the only way they can decipher for themselves what is real, what is good, what is evil, what is right, and what is wrong through the Word of God.

The Breastplate of Righteousness

The breastplate of righteousness is one of the greatest weapons of defense. It is where the heart is. We need to protect our hearts at all costs. The Scriptures say, *"Out of the abundance of the heart, the mouth speaks."* Therefore, since this is the case, all manners of evil are devised in the heart. The Bible says the heart is so wicked and deceitful that no man can know the depth of it except God. Also all the issues of life flow from the heart. So, it is very important to guard our heart.

Therefore, we are to protect ourselves by doing what is righteous before God. We are righteous in God's sight because of what Jesus did on the cross.

When you teach your children to walk in righteousness before the righteous God, it shows itself as a weapon of defense against all the strategies of Satan.

Having a heart after God and obeying all He commands is, in essence, the breastplate of righteousness because it does not allow the fiery darts to penetrate the heart.

The heart is important in the spiritual walk because either we will bow our heart to God or to man. Our very life depends on the condition of the heart.

No wonder God gave us an entire breastplate of righteous to cover our heart. Let me explain. A roman soldier put on his breastplate to protect himself from the weapons of the enemy. One key area it protected was the heart. It is the heart that pumps blood throughout our circulatory system. Without this happening, we wouldn't be alive.

Now, do you understand the importance of the breastplate of righteousness? It protects the heart. If you injure the heart, the body dies.

If you don't protect your heart from spiritual harm, you will spiritually die.

Shoes of Strength

We stand with our feet strong and firmly planted. We become unmoved by any threat made against by the enemy and unmoved by the lies he speaks, standing with our feet grounded no matter how tough, rough, or scary things may look in the heat of the battle.

We are standing strong, knowing that God will deliver us if we don't give up and faint. Satan is under our feet. We teach our children that after they have stood up under the enemy's tactics, *"the God of peace shall bruise Satan under your feet shortly. The grace of our Lord Jesus Christ be with you. Amen"* (Romans 16:20KJV). That is what the Word of God tells us.

Let me explain why some historians believe the Roman army won over their enemies; they believe it is due to their footwear. Their footwear had spikes on the soles. This was ingenious because it provided them with a strong stance and balance, which meant they had a great posture in the heat of the battle, especially on hills and uneven ground. Because of their position and attitude, knowing they would not be easily trampled or fall over, they were able to fight even in the worst places.

This is what we need to teach our children. They must stand with their feet planted on the Word of God because the Word of God will never fail them, especially during difficult and challenging times. They need to stand strong and see the salvation of their God.

Shield of Faith

In addition to all these, take the Christian faith as your shield. With it, you can put out all the flaming arrows of the evil one.

The shield is what protects the arrows flying towards a soldier. Faith is believing God will take care of them regardless of what storm they find themselves in.

God says He is in the fire, and He is in the eye of the storm. He was there in the boat with the disciples, and He came walking on the water when the disciples were caught in the eye of the storm. It is the faith we have in Christ, and in the midst of their battles, they must keep the faith.

The Scriptures say that faith comes through hearing the Word of God. We need to speak the Word of God to our children as much as possible.

The Roman shield was not like we understand shields to be. Let me explain. It was long and rectangular, and it went from the knees up to the chin. That was quite a shield, big enough to protect them from the arrows and spears. The other interesting fact is that they could kneel behind this protective shield during a barrage of arrows in the heat of the battle. It was designed to give the soldiers strength and flexibility, and it protected their heads as well.

Satan does battle in the head. That's his battleground. Teaching our children scriptures on faith is a matter of life or death in a trial. Faith says that no matter what they know, God will take care of them.

Faith wins all the time.

The Helmet of Salvation

Also take salvation as your helmet. We teach that our children are saved through Jesus Christ. This is what we must get into their mind. The helmet is what protects the head.

Satan uses the mind of people as his battleground. Therefore, we teach our children that they belong to God. A child of a king is protected at all costs. Our children are the children of the highest King. We are saved from all harm.

Every time my children are battling something, I refer to Philippians 4:8(KJV), *"Finally, brethren, whatsoever things are true, whatsoever things are honest, whatsoever things are just, whatsoever things are pure, whatsoever things are lovely, whatsoever things are of good report; if there be any virtue, and if there be any praise, think on these things."*

Let me explain how important this is. When we were building our home, I took a permanent marker, and wrote Bible verses on the walls of every room and on the concrete floors, especially where the bedframes would be, so that my children's minds will be protected by the Word of God that was written on the walls. Their feet would walk on scriptures I had written on the concrete. This may sound crazy to some people, but this was a demonstration of the faith we had in God and in His Word.

The Sword of the Spirit

The Word of God is the sword the Spirit. It is the sword that cuts to pieces. It slays and it destroys. The Word of God is what tears down, kills, and destroys all lies and all evil. Hebrews 4:12 says, *"For the word of God is quick, and powerful, and sharper than any two-edged sword, piercing even to the dividing asunder of soul and spirit, and of the joints and marrow, and is a discerner of the thoughts and intents of the heart."* Do you see that? The Word of God is the sword of the Spirit.

We absolutely, without a doubt, must teach our children to speak the Word of God. I tell my children, "Speak Bible." It's the only language their mother understands. I have a reason for saying that. Because in everything we do, we are showcasing what we know about the Word of God. Our tongue has the power of life and death.

I will cut my children's sentences off when I hear something negative coming out of their mouths. Please understand I am a mother who is raising my children in the fear and admonition of the Lord. Therefore, as it is any parent's responsibility, I must teach my children to speak life, not death. I must teach them to speak positive, not negative. That doesn't mean we deny reality, but we look to God and speak what God wants us to speak no matter what the situation or circumstance.

Parents reading this book must understand this concept because you want your children to look at things the way God wants them to and see themselves as God sees them. For example, when my daughter was 9 years old, she started to see colors in one of her eyes. She woke me up at midnight to tell me she closed her eyes and could see all these colors in one eye.

There was nothing I could do because it was midnight, so I started praying. I called a friend of mine who was a doctor, and I told him what was happening. He told me not to worry, and there was no emergency at that moment. The next morning, I called the pediatrician, and that same day, a few hours later, she went to an ophthalmologist. She was diagnosed as legally blind in that eye.

The only thing she could see was the first two lines on the eyechart. I started to panic and cry inside of me. Ellianna started to cry. Immediately, God told me that He was going to heal her eye.

I asked what could be done, but nothing could be done. I got into the car and told my little girl, "Ellianna, you will see from that eye because God said so." I got home, and I asked, "God, what do I do?"

I received a phone call from the ophthalmologist. She said there was an experimental exercise and I should call Massachusetts Eye and Ear.

My spirit leaped inside of me. I told Ellianna that God was going to heal her eye. I told her to start thanking God for her healing. I had given Ellianna all she needed in the biblical instruction about faith. Even as a 9-year-old, she understood the concept of faith because I had been teaching her all along.

Next, we went to meet with the researcher and clinical director of this experimental therapy. She told us Ellianna was too old for this study because they had not seen anyone her age succeed.

I told them I didn't care, and that God had sent me there. I was willing to pay out of pocket. We went there every week for an entire year. Guess what? With glasses, Ellianna could read like any other normal person. I said that was amazing.

They couldn't believe Ellianna, at that age, was able to heal the eye with no medicine and no operations. She had been the first. I then asked God, "Is this what You meant by healing her? That she would be able to see with eyeglasses but still remain legally blind without her eyeglasses?"

God responded, "I told you I am healing her eye." Two years later, Ellianna developed severe headaches. I called the pediatrician immediately, and I told her that I was scared and needed Ellianna seen that day.

The pediatrician made a special phone call for Ellianna to see a specialist that same day. When Ellianna showed up for the appointment, they gave her an eye test without the glasses. Ellianna could not only see from that blind eye but was able to read 18/20. The technician stopped and asked Ellianna if she was reading from the good eye. She wasn't. She immediately called the doctor and told the doctor to come over because Ellianna could see from the blind eye. The doctor said, "This is a medical miracle. We have no explanation for this. Ellianna, you are very lucky."

Those were the doctor's words. I don't believe in luck, but I do believe in God's blessing. Then she continued and told my daughter, "Ellianna, you will have no problem now getting a driver's license. You are no longer legally blind in that eye."

What a mighty God we serve. You see, Satan came to attack. I spoke the Word of God over my daughter and taught her to do the same. Then, I followed what the medical community had to say and did what they said. I didn't give up when I was told the treatment didn't work on children her age. I listened to another voice, the voice of the Holy Spirit, who said, "Do this treatment anyway."

Obedience is better than sacrifice, and what we speak forth is yes and amen when it is led by the Holy Spirit.

The Roman soldiers' sword was not an ordinary one. It was, in fact, a two-edge sword with the end turned upward. This kind of sword inflicts more severe and lethal damage than just a regular sword. This sword was designed to kill. It could rip the enemy's insides to shreds. It was so powerful that it only needed to go two to three inches into a person. It caused a fatal wound.

The sword had a huge advantage because it was double-sided, able to cut in two directions. This is how we need to approach Satan, our enemy. No wonder God describes His Word as a double-edged sword. Did you catch that? God's Word is our power, and it must come forth from our lips and tongue.

Praying in the Spirit

Pray in the Spirit in every situation. Use every kind of prayer and request there is. For the same reason, be alert. Use every kind of effort and make every kind of request for all of God's people.

We must teach our children about the role of the Holy Spirit. Because the Bible says speaking in tongues is the gift given to us by the Holy Spirit, speaking in tongues is important when it comes to prayer. The Spirit prays about things we do not know. It is here where the war is fought and won.

Through prayer, we bring to God all of our requests. He answers us according to His will.

PRAYER:

Heavenly Father, You are the God Who has armed Your children for battle. You have strengthened our arms for war. With You, we can crush an army and scale a wall.

You, O God, have gone before us. You are our Commander In Chief. Thank You for going before us.

Through You, we can do great exploits, and we shall do valiantly.

Lord, You have provided us with the armor of God and equipped us with Your Word. Help us to teach our children how to do warfare the way You have commanded.

Help us to teach our children how to put on every piece of the armor You have provided.

Lord God, I join the readers in praying over our children as we incorporate the truth we have learned through Your Word in this book.

May we stand our ground and determine to bring up a generation of godly children who will bring forth the next generation of godly children.

May we see all of the generations that come from us be men and women of valor because of how we trained our own children.

Let us be living, active demonstrations for our children on how to use the sword of the Spirit and how to put on the whole armor of God.

Lord, help us to get our children to understand they can only be successful and be victorious when they are rooted in You and grounded in Your Word, that they must be living in obedience to You.

Equip our children for battle so they can stand upon You and fight the fiery arrows of the enemy.

Lord, hold up our children by Your victorious right hand and make them victors in Christ, victorious in the battles that come their way.

Teach our children they need only to stand their ground in You and You will fight for them.

May they always remember to be still and know You are God.

In Jesus' name, Amen.

THINK ABOUT IT:

What practical ways can you implement discipline for your children in this area?

Write out a prayer, specifically for your children, about this area of discipline.

ACKNOWLEDGMENTS

I want to thank my publisher, Rise UP Publications, for asking me to write this book.

Thank you to my executive director and copyeditor, Linda A. Knowles, at Thread of Hope, Inc. for all her hard work.

To my children, Justin and Ellianna, for using their lives to teach me important truths about living a godly and blessed life.

Thank you to Mary Laity, my layout and graphic designer, who constantly blesses me with her amazing talents and eye for beautiful artwork.

Finally, and most importantly, thank you to my Lord and Savior Jesus Christ, who gives me wisdom and understanding to use my words to build the kingdom of God.

RIGHTEOUS LIVING
A BLESSED LIFE

Do you want to experience the blessings of God in your life? Do you want to see miracles worked in your family? Do you want God to hear and answer your prayers? If you have answered yes to all those questions, then there is only one way to do this; that is by living a righteous life before God.

This means obeying His Word. This means being holy as He is holy. There is no neutral ground when it comes to living for God. You are either living for Him or not.

Psalm 34:17(KJV) says, "The righteous cry, and the LORD heareth, and delivereth them out of all their troubles." God is so gracious, so kind, and so merciful that He hears the cries of the righteous.

He doesn't just hear them, but He delivers them out of all their troubles. The Hebrew word "natsal" is transliterated into the English word "delivereth," meaning "rescue, save." Did you catch that? God is going to rescue and save you from all those things which came to destroy you. He will make a way of escape in each and every situation that was meant to harm you. If that doesn't make you want to live a righteous life, I pray, as you study and discover the lives of the men and women in this book, that you are encouraged, spurred on, and desire to grow in righteousness.

Job, the most righteous man who ever lived, said, "Though he slay me yet will I trust him." This is what it means: Job was a righteous man who had done no wrong, and tragedy after tragedy happened to him in a short amount of time. Yet, God allowed it, but the victory became Job's victory.

God heard Job's prayer in his stricken state. God healed and restored Job, and God gave him double what he had lost.

So it shall be with you and me as His Word states. Whatever the cry of your heart is, you can be sure God hears you. He sees your tears, and He can't bear to see His children in pain, distress, or heartache.

He already has a plan of action to deliver you as we will see in the lives the people in this book. The Never-ending Oil of the Widow and Her Sons, The Courageous Abigail, The Mighty Warrior Caleb, and Faithful Noah. These were all righteous people who had calamities and tragedies happen to them, had people who opposed them, and dealt with those who tried to stop their blessing. However, it was the Lord who delivered them out of all their troubles...

Available in Paperback and eBook from Your Favorite Bookstore or Online Retailer

ALSO BY REV. DR. TERESA CITRO

Raising Righteous Children

Righteous Living

ABOUT THE AUTHOR

Rev. Dr. Teresa Allissa Citro is an accomplished author in the field of education and special education.

She has received many awards for her contributions in the field of special education worldwide.

Dr. Citro is the Chief Executive Officer of Learning Disabilities Worldwide Inc. and the Founder and President of Thread of Hope Inc.

In addition, she is the Founder and Chief Executive Officer of Citro Cosmetics and Skin Care, and the Founder and Chief Executive Officer of Citro Collection Fine Jewelry.

Dr. Citro is Editor and Chief of *Everyday Life Magazine*. She is the Co-Editor of two peer-reviewed journals on special education.

Dr. Citro is a worldwide public speaker.

She resides in Boston, Massachusetts, and is the mother of two children.

www.threadofhope.org

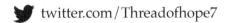 twitter.com/Threadofhope7

CPSIA information can be obtained
at www.ICGtesting.com
Printed in the USA
BVHW032101300321
603757BV00003B/20